Eighteen Weeks and a Fight for Life

Transforming Hope

By Steve Donald

malcolm down

PUBLISHING

British Library Cataloguing in Publication Data
A catalogue record for this book is available from the British Library.

ISBN 978-1-917455-20-6

Cover design by Esther Kotecha
Art direction by Sarah Grace

Printed in the UK

Contents

Dedication

I dedicate this memoir to my amazing wife and soulmate, Gloria, to our two daughters, Lizzie and Abi, and our three grandsons, Reuben, Fred and Theo. I also dedicate it to the brilliant staff at the Peritoneal Malignancy Unit at Basingstoke Hospital and to our wonderful family and friends, who all helped sustain us through eighteen weeks and a fight for life.

This book shows how Gloria and I found strength not just to cope but to flourish under these extreme pressures, because of our faith in the God of the Bible. This is a powerful testimony that spirituality, specifically Christianity, can provide powerful resources in health care.

CHAPTER ONE

Midwife Gets a Taste of Her Own Medicine

'I want to live,' said Gloria. 'I want to spend time with you, Steve, in our retirement and to see our three lovely grandsons grow up.'

'Well then,' I replied, 'let's see what can be done.'

The fight was on and what a tremendous battle it would be. Audrey, one of our closest friends, described Gloria as 'one tough cookie'. She would need to be and so would I. In our thirty-nine years of marriage we had faced many tests, but we were about to face the toughest test of all as Gloria's life hung in the balance. Sometimes life can be one big fight to survive.

I met Gloria in 1982 in Lancaster, when she returned from being a missionary nurse in Uganda during the fall of the evil dictator Idi Amin and went to Lancaster to train as a midwife. Gloria had been my right arm in incredibly challenging parish ministry as a vicar for thirty-four years and I had retired at Easter 2022. Gloria had fallen and broken her shoulder in four places on Tuesday 13th February 2021 during the pandemic and this was pinned and plated. It seemed to set off a sequence of health issues, like the collapse of a line of dominoes. A few weeks after falling Gloria had an operation to remove her appendix, and then a few months later had been diagnosed with bowel cancer. She had operations at Carlisle and two lots of brutal chemotherapy. The cancer had travelled to a lymph node by the aorta, and she was referred to Newcastle where she had a major operation, which was successful, in March 2022. She was declared clear of the lymph cancer, but a tiny speck was picked up by a PET scan in the peritoneum, the lining of the stomach. She was referred to Basingstoke Hospital, in south-central England, which had the best results in Europe for this kind of cancer.

So, Gloria and I, full of hope despite the ordeal of the last two years, made our way down to Basingstoke in June 2023, for life-saving surgery with a 20-30 per cent chance of a full cure, which would only become clear after five years of scans. Since retiring, my diary had been filled not with parish but hospital appointments. Over my thirty-four years as a vicar I had experienced the full range of emotions, from joy to heartache, sometimes in the same day. Gloria shared fully in those joys and heartaches. Now, we were going to experience the emotional roller coaster of eighteen weeks, and a fight for life.

Gloria was like Ruth in the Old Testament of the Bible. Like the Ruth of that wonderful story, she was loyal and devoted. When we were engaged in 1983, just as Gloria was taking her midwifery exams, she gave me a new Bible with the famous inscription from Ruth 1:16-17:

Where you go I will go, and where you stay I will stay. Your people will be my people and your God my God. Where you die I will die, and there I will be buried. May the LORD deal with me, be it ever so severely, if even death separates you and me.

Our faith in God was about to be tested as never before during an intense period of eighteen weeks. What this story will show is that our faith was real and strong. We felt the weakest as human beings but the strongest as Christians. Both surgeons – Gloria's surgeon at the Royal Victoria Institute in Newcastle and Alex at Basingstoke Hospital – replied when I said we were Christians who believed in the power and love of God and that many Christians were praying for Gloria, that there is considerable data and evidence that having a faith improves outcomes and helps holistically with the health of the patient and their relatives. In this memoir I want to tell the story of how we found strength from the God revealed in the Bible and reflect on the importance of spirituality in health care in these days of rapid cultural change.

What is our cultural context from a Christian perspective? Tom Holland, the popular historian who wrote *Dominion*, considers Christianity to be in the air we breathe yet society has moved away from these foundations. He writes:

To live in a Western country is to live in a society still utterly saturated by Christian concepts and assumptions

7

. . . The West, increasingly empty though the pews may be, remains firmly moored to its Christian path.[1]

These concepts and assumptions, often referred to as doctrines, were made personal and transformative for Gloria and me through a personal encounter with, and a living faith in, Jesus Christ. It is a tragic mistake to separate doctrine and life; the Bible always holds them together. This is one of the key reasons why the pews are empty.

I want to tell a positive story of how a genuine and living faith in Christ helped Gloria and me to get through and indeed flourish through the most extreme of pressures at Basingstoke Hospital. Victor Frankl, a psychiatrist, wrote of his experiences in a Nazi concentration camp, 'Man is not destroyed by suffering; he is destroyed by suffering without meaning.'[2]

Religion and spirituality still form the foundation of meaning for many people, especially of our age group. There is considerable research to back this up and you can find examples of this in the appendix at the end of the book. So, it will be a memoir on a topic which I think engages with many people today and will tell a very positive story of Gloria's and my experience of doctors, nurses, physios, psychologists, chaplains and others at Basingstoke Hospital, and the pastoral care provided by the local church at St Mary's, Basingstoke, giving meaning and tremendous support to Gloria and me as we faced arguably the biggest challenge of our lives, to suffer well and with meaning and purpose. Our family and

---

1. Tom Holland, *Dominion* (London: Little, Brown, 2019), p. xxv.
2. https://bmcpalliatcare.biomedcentral.com/articles/10.1186/s12904-022-01116-x quoting V.E. Frankl, *Man's Search for Meaning* (New York: Simon and Schuster, 1984).

friends across many church fellowships would also play an incredibly significant role. Using the benefits of social media we became a suffering community of almost daily updates and fervent prayer and praise. Our suffering brought us together with an even stronger bond.

This is a story and subject that will connect with many people, those with faith and those with none (although everyone has a worldview that shapes their lives). I want to show how helpful a spirituality, specifically Christianity, which is in the air we breathe, can come to our aid as we face the most testing of experiences when our very lives hang in the balance. The Christian faith offers the resources we need to make sense of a crazy world in general and it addresses the unreal world of intense suffering. During our eighteen weeks in Basingstoke Hospital, I found myself continually returning to Paul's letter to the Romans, and especially chapter 5 which speaks about suffering. James chapter 1 also follows the same pattern as Romans chapter 5 towards maturity in Christ and joy in suffering.

How does Romans chapter 5 explain God's good purpose in allowing suffering? Through suffering our faith is tested by God to enable us to develop in Christian character. Knowing God the Father, through being justified by faith, we have peace with God through our Lord Jesus Christ, and we then have access to the grace of God (Romans 5:1-2). This enables us to rejoice in the hope of the glory of God and to rejoice in our sufferings because suffering produces perseverance; perseverance, character; and character, hope (verses 3-4). These verses and the experience of their daily reality are at the heart of this book and how Gloria and I spiritually and mentally prospered under the most unimaginable pressure.

When our first child was born we named her Elizabeth Ruth, since, as I have said, the story of Ruth resonates with our story. Gloria was a midwife at Lancaster Infirmary and because our daughter was born on New Year's Day, the story and their photographs appeared in the local newspaper in January 1986. The headline ran, 'Midwife gets a taste of her own medicine.' In a sense, history was repeating itself as both Gloria and I were 'getting a taste of our own medicine' as we began our eighteen weeks at Basingstoke Hospital. Gloria on the ward and me in the nearby hospital accommodation kindly provided for patients' relatives by the National Health Service. Instead of being the medic giving nursing care, Gloria was on the receiving end of it, and it is a well-known fact that medics make the most challenging of patients! I would add that its far easier in my experience for a vicar to give spiritual help than receive it. How would we both get on with this – the greatest challenge of our lives? What we both found was that having a faith in God and belonging to his living Church came to our rescue and enabled us not only to survive but overcome in this titanic struggle – eighteen weeks and a fight for life. Our story will show the importance of spirituality in health care and point to spiritual resources that can give meaning and purpose to our suffering.

CHAPTER TWO

One Tough Cookie

Most of this story will be set in a Basingstoke Hospital bed, but Gloria was obviously more than a patient. Who was Gloria Donald and what did she do for the sixty-nine years before we came to Basingstoke Hospital in June 2023?

Gloria was born in St Helens in 1953 and grew up with two sisters and two brothers on a tough housing estate. After the tragic death of her father in an accident at the bus depot where he was a driver, her mum Joan had to bring up the family on her own. Jackie, Gloria's younger sister, told me that when there was a gap between wallpapering the bedroom they shared, Gloria drew a large picture of a ballerina on the wall. This was her dream to be a ballerina when she grew up.

Aged fifteen she heard from attending her local church, St John's, Ravenhead, that Jesus had died for her on the cross and that if she had been the only person needing Jesus to die for them he would have done it, just for her. She decided to follow Jesus Christ. She read about the missionary heroine Gladys Aylward, made famous in 1958 by the film starring

Ingrid Bergman, *The Inn of the Sixth Happiness*. Sadly, this film took many liberties and was far from the truth, which was even more exciting! Gloria read an excellent and much more accurate version that inspired her to become a missionary, *A London Sparrow: The Story of Gladys Aylward* by Phyllis Thompson, published in 1971. I have the very copy dated by Gloria herself as 1971 and the reference she wrote to Proverbs 3:5-6, which says:

> *Trust in the LORD with all your heart and lean not on your own understanding; in all your ways submit to him, and he will make your paths straight.*

This truth and the story of Gladys Aylward became the inspiration for her future life as a missionary. Gloria returned in 1981 from missionary work, fulfilling her calling serving for eighteen months in a bush hospital in Northern Uganda. Her first patient had been a small boy called Samuel who had fallen from a tree on to a stake. His parents arrived at the hospital and Gloria asked them when the accident had happened. They replied, 'Three days ago.'

'Why didn't you bring him sooner?' Gloria asked.

'We have been carrying him for three days,' they replied.

Samuel survived the fall but died two weeks later of measles. His parents said he was vaccinated for measles, but Gloria thought the vaccine may have gone off because of the heat. Gloria, Bill and Judy Cave (Bill was a doctor) and their two children had flown into a war zone to reach the hospital in 1979 as Idi Amin fled the country after ordering an invasion of neighbouring Tanzania. When our friend Audrey called Gloria 'one tough cookie', she was right. One night two Ugandans were having a fight with machetes, and one almost sliced the ear off the other. The headman (responsible for security in the hospital and for emergencies) put his spear through the window of Gloria's bedroom with a note on it. It read, 'Sister, come quick to the hospital.' Gloria dressed quickly and went to see what was going on. When she assessed the situation she went outside of the home of Bill and Judy Cave and through their open ground-floor bedroom window asked Bill to come. Bill was tucked up comfortably in bed and asked Gloria what her needlework skills were like. Gloria said she was rather good. 'Well then,' said Bill, 'see what you can do yourself.' Gloria stitched on the ear and the 'operation' was a complete success.

When Idi Amin fled the country, elections were called to elect a new president of Uganda. The local Christian headmaster, Christopher, was asked to oversee that the elections in the village were fair and free. Whilst voting took place he noticed that certain men and women were trying to vote more than once, so he would put a tiny pencil mark on their birth certificates, which they brought with them as proof of identity. When the opposition party heard that he was turning away their fraudulent supporters they issued a call for him to be killed. When Gloria and her housemate heard about this they hid Christopher in their house for two weeks until things calmed down. Gloria was one tough cookie.

Returning to England in 1981 she trained for midwifery in London. When I read her school reports, the headmaster had written, 'Gloria is highly intelligent and could do well if she can overcome her "examinationitus".' Having failed the midwifery exam several times in London, in desperation she wrote to the Head of Midwifery at Lancaster Infirmary to ask for a final chance. Elizabeth Swarbrick, who had herself been a missionary nurse in Uganda, warmed to Gloria's story and invited her for interview and she joined the course. With Elizabeth's instruction and confidence-building approach (and my encouragement), out of a class of eight, Gloria came top and won a special award with her name inscribed on a plaque in the hospital. We got married in 1984 and Elizabeth Ruth (as already mentioned) was born in 1986 while we were in Lancaster, and Abigail Rachel in 1987, when we were at Oak Hill Theological College where I was training as a vicar.

I had gone to teacher training college in Liverpool in 1973 and became a Christian in 1974 after reading John's gospel and joining the local Anglican church. Gloria had Gladys Aylward to inspire her. One of my Christian heroes is Eric Liddell, made famous in my generation by the 1981 film *Chariots of Fire*. (It was the only time I ever saw my dad jog, as he and my two brothers imitated the famous scene running across the beach to that iconic music.) At the 1924 Paris Olympics, Eric Liddell refused to run on the Sabbath in the heats of the 100 metres race in which he was tipped to win gold, and instead ran in the 400 metres final he had not trained for. Incredibly, running in that distinctive head-leant-back style he won gold to wide acclaim.

The son of missionary parents born in China, he went back to his missionary work instead of pursuing further sporting success. On a human level what then happened to Eric Liddell seems quite tragic. When the Japanese invaded China, Liddell sent his pregnant wife Florence and two daughters to safety in Canada. Interned in a squalid prison camp without running water and working sanitation, Eric died of an undiagnosed brain tumour aged just forty-three. As Christians we have a distinct perspective on suffering since we know of its redemptive power in the death of Christ but also how it can transform our lives. Many Christians would know Romans 8:28, 'And we know that in all things God works for the good of those who love him, who have been called according to his purpose.' In Eric Liddell's desperate circumstances, he was able to help many children in the camp with sports coaching and refereeing. He tempered his earlier strong stance against playing sport on the Sabbath when he found that the children of the camp, without his refereeing, were fighting. He clearly thought helping these poor children get through a terrible ordeal was more important than his personal scruples. One of the children, who later became a pastor, commented that Liddell was 'Jesus Christ in running shoes', but Liddell himself stressed the importance of giving all the glory to his Lord and Saviour Jesus Christ. Gloria and I did not have the worldwide fame of a Gladys Aylward or an Eric Liddell but as Christians we would say the same as these two humble servants of Christ. As Eric Liddell put it, 'When you speak of me, give the glory to my master, Jesus Christ.' Gladys Aylward wrote something remarkably similar.

I was, by this time, feeling very much alone – a small, strange woman in a very foreign land. But in spite of this, there was a great peace in my heart as I looked back on all God had done for me so far. I truly believed He intended me to get to China to work for Him there.[3]

Gloria was an ordinary woman who did extraordinary things. She, like Aylward and Liddell, would say it was Christ living in and through her. When I was at a Bible school called Capernwray (which is what brought me to Lancaster and that's how Gloria and I met), I heard a talk from Major Ian Thomas, a popular Christian speaker of the 20th century, on the subject of Moses and the burning bush in Exodus chapter 3 (made famous by Charlton Heston in the epic Hollywood film *The Ten Commandments*). Speaking of how this story signifies Christ empowering the ordinary Christian to live an extraordinary life, since the bush did not burn up, he said, 'Any bush will do!' You will hear in this memoir how Christ living through ordinary people, like Gloria and me, could suffer well as Christians, because the power came from Christ and 'any bush will do'. Whether you have a faith in God or none, I hope you will find this an inspiring story of faith and courage in extreme adversity.

Gloria had her own share of suffering, sadness and disappointment in her life. She responded in faith to the death of her dad and the hostility of her mum, who made it so that Gloria was unable to leave the family home to pursue a nursing career until she was eighteen. Despite this adversity, Gloria's faith grew in maturity as Romans 5 and James 1 describe. She began witnessing to her family, putting Christian tracts and books where her mum could find them and living a

3. Gladys Aylward with Christine Hunter, *Gladys Aylward, My Missionary Life in China* (Chicago: Moody, 1970) p. 21.

consistent Christian life, despite much opposition. Eventually many members of her family came to Christ, including her mum, her sister and younger brother, as well as many aunties and uncles. Gloria patiently trusted her Saviour for her vision of becoming first a qualified nurse, then a missionary nurse in Uganda and then a midwife in England.

Whilst we sadly live in a Western culture that is largely turning its back on its Christian roots, on the Christianity that the popular author Tom Holland says in his book *Dominion* is in the air we breathe, it still retains its ability to empower the weak and transform bleak and dark circumstances. It enables ordinary people to do extraordinary things that point to the fact we are more than flesh and bone, and that Jesus is alive and very much at work in this world for those with eyes to see.

CHAPTER THREE

The Midland Hotel and Our Wedding Anniversary

Throughout my fifty years as a Christian and thirty-nine years of Christian marriage, meeting countless people of all sorts of background and belief, one common factor has been clear. Everyone I have ever spoken to in any kind of depth has had the same deep purpose to their lives, often below the surface but clearly expressed by what they said about themselves. What is the common desire of every human being on the planet? It is to be happy. Happiness is often related to 'happenings'. If our lives go smoothly and well, we are happy, but if we face discouragement and disappointment, we are unhappy. How should we look at life with a Christian mind? The Bible, and particularly Romans chapter 5 which we have been examining, speaks of a deep joy from knowing Christ, which is not tied to 'happenings' but to the transforming relationship of knowing Christ as our hope. Describing how we 'rejoice in hope of the glory of God' (knowing God in Christ, the purpose for which we were made), Paul then says:

Not only that, but we rejoice in our sufferings, knowing that suffering produces endurance, and endurance produces character, and character produces hope, and hope does not put us to shame, because God's love has been poured into our hearts through the Holy Spirit who has been given to us.

(Romans 5:3-5 ESV)

This joy in the Holy Spirit was most clearly seen in the life of Christ. Whilst Christ's life was full of suffering and Isaiah speaks of him as being 'a man of sorrows, and acquainted with grief' (Isaiah 53:3 KJV), he was sustained by a deep joy. In Hebrews 12:1-2 the writer gives us his exhortation to 'fix our eyes on Jesus, the author and perfecter of our faith' and then gives us the motivation of Christ to suffer: 'for the joy set before him' (the joy of saving from sin and death those he would call to himself), 'endured the cross, scorning its shame, and sat down at God's right hand.'

The Midland Hotel is one of the iconic images of Morecambe which Gloria and I called our local, where we often had coffee whilst admiring the amazing floating staircase featured in the classic TV series *Poirot*, played by David Suchet, based on the stories by Agatha Christie. The other iconic image of our town is the statue of Eric Morecambe (of the UK popular comedy duo Morecambe and Wise) on the promenade. In this exact spot, when there were small shelters along the promenade (before the statue of Eric), I proposed to Gloria in 1983. The town will have a new iconic image and a source of economic and cultural transformation when the Eden Project is built on the promenade round the back of the Midland Hotel. In 2023 the project was awarded £50 million by the levelling-up fund and awaits matching funding by local businesses, Lancaster Council and local donors. It will make an enormous difference to the area as well as the town, bringing more investment and giving Morecambe a distinctive identity since its heyday as a seaside resort. What it has always retained is an amazing view across the Great Bay and some sensational sunsets.

During our long and happy marriage, life had not always been sunny. The Lord had led us through several painful experiences in ministry. As our dear friend of many years, Esther Barratt, summed it up well when I retired as a vicar in 2022: 'I tell people you had a series of very difficult parishes with a whole range of challenging folk, but you have come through.' These experiences had left some deep scars and bruises, but we were sustained by 'the joy of the LORD [which] is your strength' (Nehemiah 8:10). Gloria had endured two years of brutal chemotherapy, just at the point when we were looking forward to a happy retirement. Our 39th wedding anniversary was especially poignant, given our recent struggles and in the light of anticipating the next challenge at Basingstoke.

For our 39th wedding anniversary I ordered a large, framed print of the Midland Hotel by Tabitha Mary, and added the inscription, 'Happy 39th Wedding Anniversary'. Gloria loved it. Throughout our incredibly happy marriage I had made anniversaries and Gloria's birthday a high priority, because I felt Gloria did so much for me and the two girls that she deserved to be spoiled on these special occasions. For our 20th wedding anniversary I had organised a surprise event at a church in York, where I had arranged for the archdeacon of York to lead a recommitment of our marriage vows and for our dear friend and mentor Revd Frank Allred, who had married us in 1984, to preach a sermon.

The secret of the planned surprise event held well for six months. I found myself telling 'white lies' to Gloria and making a secret visit to check out the hotel. I had engaged Gloria's sister Jackie for the invitation replies to go to her address, and I had involved our dear friends Revd Don and Mrs Audrey Andrew in using their church for the service and their hall for the reception. We had the same hymns as we had at our 1984 wedding. I had planned to get Gloria to the church on a ruse on the actual day, until the archdeacon wisely counselled me to tell her the night before, which I did in the Blue Bridge Hotel in York. On the Friday night, before the anniversary the next day, we bumped into our friends David and Di Bayley, who had provided the bungalow on Anglesey for our honeymoon. David was under the reasonable impression that Gloria still did not know why we were in York and produced an impressive cover story of why they were there themselves, i.e. he said they had visited the York Railway Museum and decided to stay over. It was so convincing that I did not like to inform him that I had just told Gloria about the surprise following the archdeacon's advice.

I also tried hard to surprise Gloria on her birthday, which was 21st November. When Gloria was pregnant with Lizzie, her Canadian friend and fellow midwife Jeanie was staying over with us in Lancaster. I had asked my good friend John Curnow, an Australian who taught Religious Education in the nearby

Skerton Secondary School, to dress up in a full-size gorilla outfit and knock on our door with some flowers for Gloria. On the day of Gloria's birthday John walked down Clarendon Road to the end of the street where we lived. He was barked at by several dogs, but managed to shake them off. The day before I heard Gloria and Jeanie discussing how shock could bring on the prompt arrival of a baby and I panicked at my plans for the next day! I confided my fears in Jeanie and she said, 'If that happens, at least I am on hand to deliver the baby!' So, John dressed as a gorilla rang the doorbell and Jeanie and I pretended not to hear so Gloria went to the door (in her dressing gown I remember), took one look at the gorilla with the flowers and, before John could say anything, slammed the door on him! Fortunately, he persisted, and she eventually opened the door and accepted the flowers without going straight into labour! When Gloria married me she said, 'I am a midwife, but now I'm a mad wife.'

I share these stories to show how much Gloria and I loved each other and how much fun it was being married to her! Amid all the struggle and pain of Christian ministry we could experience a deep joy, which was often expressed in laughter. Audrey tells the story of how whilst she and Don were at a parish in the Isle of Man, Gloria rang up pretending to be a Scouse lady (Scouse refers to a local dish and people from Liverpool are called 'Scousers', who have a very distinctive accent), looking for accommodation. On another occasion at a strawberry garden party, Gloria vowed to eat the largest strawberry you have ever seen in one go, and she did! As well as being one tough cookie, Gloria was very funny.

We have already seen how Gloria's life, before we met and married and then subsequently in our Christian marriage, followed the pattern of faith in Christ leading to perseverance, and perseverance to hope. James chapter 1 follows the same pattern as Romans chapter 5: the testing of faith leading to perseverance, and perseverance leading to character – or as James has it, maturity in Christ. This was one of the things that drew Gloria and me together, our mutual love for God. James uses a striking statement before outlining this pattern, which in eighteen intense weeks at Basingstoke Hospital was to be tested and proved in the fires of deep pain, disappointment and struggle.

> *Count it all joy, my brothers and sisters, when you meet trials of various kinds, for you know that the testing of your faith produces steadfastness. And let steadfastness have its full effect, that you may be perfect and complete, lacking in nothing.*
>
> (James 1:2-4 ESV)

In 1988, whilst at what I call 'vicar factory' (Oak Hill Theological College in London), I read a life-transforming book by John Piper called *Desiring God*. It came out originally in 1986 and was updated with a new chapter on suffering in 2003. Piper coined a new term, 'Christian Hedonism', and its key principle is that 'God is most glorified in me, when I am most satisfied in Him'.[4]

He took the Westminster Confession of Faith, written by godly Puritans, and changed a couple of words because of his study

---

4.   John Piper, *Desiring God*, (Colorado: Multnomah Books, 1986, 2003) p. 288.

of Scripture. The Confession reads: 'The chief end of man is to glorify God and enjoy him forever.' Piper changed it by substituting 'by' instead of 'and', and by changing 'enjoy' to 'enjoying'. His version reads: 'The chief end of man is to glorify God *by* enjoying him forever.'[5]

This life-transforming insight, which is expressed in James 1:2, 'Count it all joy . . . when you meet trials of various kinds', was to be tested and proved by eighteen weeks and a fight for life in Basingstoke Hospital.

5. Ibid p. 18.

CHAPTER FOUR

D-Day at Basingstoke

Week One

On Tuesday 6th June 2023 we drove down from our apartment in Morecambe to Basingstoke to begin the greatest fight of our lives. Strangely, Gladys Aylward, Gloria's early inspiration at eighteen to become a missionary, returned from China to England when the Communists took over in 1945, and lived out most of the rest of her life in Basingstoke. The town grew as an overflow to London in the 1960s and is known as 'doughnut city' because of its many roundabouts. When I went to a church conference in Nairobi in 2014, I met briefly the then rector of St Mary's, Basingstoke, so when we were going to the town I thought I would try this church on my first Sunday morning, since I knew it would teach the Bible and be a lively church. My plan for my own mental and spiritual health was twofold: first to get support from the local church, adding to the already substantial prayer support from family, friends and our own church family back in Carnforth; and second to use a psychological method of distraction by having a project to focus my mind on positively, whilst Gloria was recovering with the inevitable ups and downs.

I had brought my desk-top computer with the plan to move on with my current writing project. We had been told it would be two to three weeks recovery time before I could take Gloria home to Morecambe, which would be a brilliant place for her convalescence and recovery. We were holding on tight to the plan of enjoying a long retirement together in the town where I had proposed and where all the memories were happy. It was also a place where we still had several close friends. We were looking forward to seeing our three grandsons grow up and spending more time with them down in Yeovil with Abi our daughter and her husband Ben, who is also a clergyman.

As I've already detailed, Gloria and I had an incredibly happy marriage for over thirty-nine years but do not think for a moment that it was perfect. I did author a book entitled *Marriages Are Made in Heaven* in 2021, which was delayed by the pandemic and came out on Valentine's Day, but we did have some serious disagreements. I used to say to wedding couples as I prepared them for marriage, that living in a detached vicarage was brilliant because you can have a noisy row and no one can hear you! My dad said we were like two peas in a pod but there was one thing we consistently disagreed about, which was my driving. I am a good driver, but Gloria was one of the world's best back-seat drivers. When she broke her shoulder and had to travel in the back I thought things would improve but they got worse. I would say, 'Gloria, I am driving, be quiet!' to no effect. Whilst I found this very annoying (and I am sure there were annoying traits in my character, like always having an excuse for everything), there were times when I was pleased about her interference, and our arrival at the hospital accommodation site was one such occasion. I was driving around the ten blocks of accommodation, most of it for hospital staff, many from the Caribbean and Africa, with patients' relatives helpfully on the ground-floor flats, with Gloria in the back seat like the Queen used to travel. I was concentrating on looking for my accommodation block and failed to see a lowered barrier when Gloria exclaimed, 'Stop the car!' I heeded the warning and strongly braked, just feet away from the barrier. If I had continued I would have done considerable damage to my car, so on this occasion I was grateful for Gloria's intervention.

The operation took place as scheduled on the Friday and halfway through the six-hour procedure our surgeon Alex rang me to say that they believed it was going well. Gloria would not need a stoma bag (which was necessary in a few cases), and that the hernia repair had gone well, and she would not need a mesh support but would be fitted with a corset. Two small lumps of cancer had been removed. Gloria had struggled with her damaged shoulder which had not fixed well as it happened during the pandemic when there was little face-to-face physio. She had also carried this large hernia, which made her feel like she was pregnant, from the big operation at Newcastle on the lymph cancer near her aorta. What Alex told me on the Friday reassured me that everything was going well.

On the Saturday Amie from Critical Care rang me to say Gloria was still on the ventilator but was doing very well with some medication and was understanding everything Amie was telling her. I went in to see her for the first time in

Critical Care and it was tough to see her on the ventilator, vastly different from a normal ward. I had visited parishioners and my auntie Joyce in Critical Care before, but it was still a shock when it is your beloved wife. Sunday's report was mixed since Gloria was having a rough day and they were trying to balance the medication, but she had come off the ventilator. Monday was worse with Gloria reporting severe pain in her shoulder and I wrote in my diary, 'I'm struggling.' On Tuesday, James, one of the Critical Care doctors, rang to say they were putting Gloria back on the ventilator. At this point I was concerned about Gloria but thought she just needed a bit of time. I was encouraged by the fact that Abi was coming on Thursday to have lunch with me in Basingstoke and then to see her mum.

As already mentioned, I had brought my desk-top computer and printer with the intention of moving on with my latest book project. This was about the massive shift of the Western Church away from the clear teaching of the Bible. I hoped to be able to advance it by a few chapters and have something to keep my mind off Gloria's sufferings. The flat, as described in the patient relatives' booklet, had small rooms that reminded me of my college accommodation, with a narrow bed and a thin mattress that I would nickname affectionately 'the prison bed', with the redeeming feature of a spacious desk and free and effective internet connection. Unfortunately, I had forgotten my keyboard and had to undergo a frustrating weekend while I waited for a second-hand one from Amazon to arrive at the accommodation office whose postcode I had been given. Promptly at 8.30am I arrived at the office on the Monday to be told that my package had not arrived and I should contact Amazon, which occupied Tuesday with no effect. Later in the day I received the text, 'package handed to a resident'. Did they know there were three hundred residents here? How was I to know which one had my keyboard?

First thing Wednesday I sat bolt upright in my prison bed and had a lightbulb moment. Each of the accommodation blocks had a glass door through which you could usually see Amazon packages delivered that day. I would work my way through the ten blocks and hopefully find my missing keyboard, so I could start work. The first block had nothing in the doorway and the second had a curtain over the door, but when I looked through the door of the third block I could see down the corridor that there was a package leaning against a door and it looked suspiciously like the shape of a keyboard! So, like in the films, I waited until a resident came out, I held the door and said, 'Good morning,' and gained access. Eureka! It was my package containing my replacement keyboard and so work could begin.

This was an important distraction that I had planned to help me cope. Whilst obviously concerned about Gloria's condition we had been through two years of major surgery and two brutal periods of chemotherapy. The surgeon at Newcastle after Gloria's recovery from her serious operation, said that Gloria had proved her 'survivorship'. For every Gloria, he said there would be a hundred who did not respond so well. She was, as Audrey said, 'a tough cookie'. The medics seemed confident that Gloria would soon improve and be moved to the C2 recovery ward. This reassured me.

The other stabilising factor was that my visit to St Mary's, Basingstoke, had been very encouraging on the Sunday morning following the operation on the Friday. At the door I was met by a very friendly Colin Barton, who took me into the large worship area (that seats over 300 people) and introduced me to his lovely wife, Chris. The church gets regular morning congregations of about 250 adults and fifty children. In the evening over a hundred attend. It was weeks before I realised that Colin was one of the church wardens, but he had taken me under his wing and I would sit with them each week and get massive emotional and spiritual help from this friendship. I was extremely impressed with the warmth of welcome, lively contemporary worship and excellent preaching based on the Bible, but thought I would only be attending for another couple of Sundays.

On Thursday 15th June I arranged for Abi to meet me at Eastrop Park and walk down the tree-lined walkway into Festival Place Shopping Centre, which was filled with a wide variety of restaurants and shops. Strangely, she had met a friend from London there only a couple of weeks before, deciding to meet somewhere halfway between their homes. Eastrop Park and Festival Place would be the go-to places with relatives and friends during these eighteen weeks.

It was good for Abi and me to meet up first and touch base before going into the Critical Care ward. I remember our visit together as a very emotional one (I am shedding a few tears as I write this). It was a new experience for Abi seeing her mum on a ventilator and unconscious. We held onto each other tightly and prayed. Christians were praying in our home church in Carnforth near Morecambe, in Abi and Ben's church in Yeovil, and around the country our friends and family were lifting Gloria up before the Lord and praying for her healing.

When you face such tough circumstances, having a Christian faith gives you God's peace in the storm and the support of the body of Christ. There is nothing like genuine Christian love and fellowship, whilst the pain and the turmoil remained. It was comforting to feel loved and supported by so many, including one church we had never visited. Being far from home in a completely new place and staying in a hospital was strange and potentially isolating, but I felt the love of Christ expressed locally and nationally. I was not alone since many others were standing with me and Gloria as we faced this storm that had been raging for two years.

CHAPTER FIVE

One Battered Babe

16 June – 29 June

The Bible says, 'Hope deferred makes the heart sick, but a longing fulfilled is a tree of life' (Proverbs 13:12).

On Friday 16th June I met with Tom Cecil, Director and Consultant Surgeon, who told me they were genuinely concerned about Gloria's condition but were holding off surgery because of the risks. He was on call that weekend so he would do the surgery if they thought that was the way forward. Now I was worried. More surgery, so soon after another serious operation? This was too much to bear, but I contacted everyone – on text, email and WhatsApp – and a huge blanket of prayer encircled Gloria and her loved ones. I felt comforted. Audrey described Gloria as 'one battered babe'.

On Saturday 17th June Tom told me that they were keeping Gloria asleep waiting for a tiny tear in the small bowel to heal itself. A scan had revealed the tear. 'How had this happened?' I asked.

'It could have been contact with fingers, instruments or even Gloria's own body during a very complex operation,' Tom replied.

Things had just taken a massive turn for the worse, but we were hopeful that this waiting strategy for Gloria's body to heal itself would work. I did not want Gloria to go back into surgery so soon, as I was aware of the risks. It was going to be a long job, it seemed, and a waiting strategy, but we clung on to hope.

Gloria was receiving excellent care, and I had found a good local church, made some new Christian friends, and was settling into the patient accommodation getting to know a lovely guy who, like me, came from the North East. We had lots of conversations about life and its purpose, and I shared with him our Christian hope. His wife was doing well. This began a period of supporting other relatives, which helped me cope with what was going on by focusing on God and on others rather than my own problems. The booklet from the Peritoneal Malignancy Institute had flagged up the value of chatting to one another, since 'people with similar experiences can often be a huge support for each other,' and I found this to be true, especially as the weeks turned into months. This was highlighted by meeting another family in the Critical Care family room. I was in the smaller of the two parallel family rooms with Abi when she popped out for a breather. Sadly, in the other larger room a family had just been faced with the terrible experience of their love one's life support being turned off. The sister of the young man came into the smaller room, and we began a conversation sharing each other's situation. When the sister discovered I was a Christian minister she asked me to go and meet her family in the other room. I was able to bring them some comfort and said a prayer with them with their agreement. When I returned to the smaller room Abi had come back and I shared their sad news, and we prayed for them. I said to Abi, 'I could get a job here' and she replied, 'Dad, it looks like you already have.' Whilst I could lean on my thirty-four years as a vicar, it brought real comfort to me to be helping others rather than dwelling on our own circumstances. I felt the weakest as a human being but the strongest as a Christian. Spirituality, specifically Christianity, helps not just the patient but the relatives.

On Sunday 18th June our grandsons came, and we consulted the senior staff at Critical Care as to whether they should see Gloria. Reuben was ten, Fred seven and Theo five. They left it up to the parents to assess the impact. Abi and Ben quickly decided it would not be helpful, but the boys were left asking lots of questions about what was happening to Grannie. When I enquired further a senior nurse provided an excellent booklet about Critical Care for children, with pictures and explanations of the various machines, like the ventilator, and boxes for them to draw a picture of Grannie. She managed to find a copy for each of them, which was great. Instead of going with them into Critical Care we took them to the local Milestones Museum about the history of transportation and industry in the area, which they really enjoyed. They got vouchers to go into the 'olde sweetshop' and get a ration of sweets, and Ben and I had a voucher for a pint of beer in the local 'olde pub'. It was great to feel my family around me like a security blanket. It was tough for the boys, and I remember Fred asking me round the back of the people carrier, when the rest of the family had got in, 'Grandad, will Grannie ever come out of hospital?'

'We are praying and hoping she will,' I replied. Love hurts but also hopes.

On Monday 19th June they moved Gloria to her own room in Critical Care because of the bacteria in the fluids that were draining out through a line due to the tear in her small bowel. The bacteria were a risk to other vulnerable patients but not to staff or relatives. On Tuesday Gloria blinked her eyes twice to show she could hear and understand what was being said to her.

On Wednesday 21st June I noted, 'Three different doctor conversations today.' Of these Rory and Kirsty separately advised me to look after my mental health. Rory said he thought it could be at least another six weeks for Gloria in hospital. 'Gloria will forget most of this, but you will remember it all. It would be good to talk to one of the hospital psychologists,' he advised. This was good advice, and I began to think about how I could best look after myself so I could continue to look after Gloria. I did speak to two of the psychologists, and they gave good support.

As well as the stress of all that was happening with Gloria, we were selling a house in Carlisle after buying an apartment in Morecambe for our retirement, partly with an interest-free bridging loan of £70,000 from a dear Christian friend. Joan was the host of the home where I led a Bible study in

Lancaster where Gloria and I met in 1982. She also sang at our wedding in 1984. Running two homes simultaneously and not being able to use them much was another pressure on me, but I found strength in my God and felt a great peace, although our savings were depleting rapidly. Throughout our marriage we always found that the Lord provided, whether it was over three-quarters of a million pounds during thirty-four years of parish ministry with three major church building projects, or for our personal family needs. My dad used to say, 'It's good raising money for the church, son, but try and make a bit for yourself!' Gladys Aylward and Eric Liddell (quoted earlier) always found the Lord to be faithful and so did we. Earlier providences of God's loving care encouraged me not to panic about the finances and that everything would be okay.

Biblical faith is like a muscle that gets stronger with use and testing, just like physical muscles. During this very testing time two passages from the Bible inspired and encouraged my faith. These were James 1 and Romans 5, where the writers outline a similar pattern when we exercise faith in the Lord. James says:

> *Consider it pure joy, my brothers and sisters, whenever you face trials of many kinds, because you know that the testing of your faith produces perseverance. Let perseverance finish its work so that you may be mature and complete, not lacking anything.*
>
> (James 1:2-4)

This is counter-intuitive, but it works. Paul says something similar:

We also glory in our sufferings, because we know that suffering produces perseverance; perseverance, character; and character, hope. And hope does not put us to shame, because God's love has been poured out into our hearts through the Holy Spirit, who has been given to us.

(Romans 5:3-5)

Christians believe that Christ lives in them and gives them power in their weakness to face great trials and overcome them, because we know Christ will return and bring in a new heaven and earth where there will be no sin and suffering. This gives us hope to keep going.

Having given up his opportunity to win the gold medal in the 1924 Paris Olympics because of his desire to please God first, in the film *Chariots of Fire* Eric Liddell is heard reading Scripture from the pulpit of a Paris church, whilst we see on the screen his heat being run in his absence. He reads from a powerful Old Testament passage about strength in weakness:

Do you not know? Have you not heard? The LORD is the everlasting God, the Creator of the ends of the earth. He will not grow tired or weary, and his understanding no one can fathom. He gives strength to the weary and increases the power of the weak. Even youths grow tired and weary, and young men stumble and fall; but those who hope in the LORD will renew their strength. They will soar on wings like eagles; they will run and not grow weary, they will walk and not be faint.

(Isaiah 40:28-31)

'Where does the power come from to run the race?' asks the actor playing Eric Liddell. He answers his own question, using the passage in Isaiah 40 he has just read, since he declares it comes from within, from the Lord, who dwells within by his Spirit. This is the common experience of the Christian, of strength in weakness. Liddell felt this inner strength when he put God before king and country and stayed true to his God-informed conscience. Later, in terrible conditions in a Japanese internment camp, at the end of his life he displayed the same power to overcome squalor and death. This is the power of the resurrection hope, which transforms how we live on earth because we have a hope of heaven.

One of the main lessons I was learning through eighteen weeks and a fight for life was that the genuine Christian life is about being part of the body of Christ, not just a solitary lone ranger. God uses his Church on earth to express his everlasting love. We were getting great support from our home church and from my adopted church in Basingstoke, St Mary's. Jackie, Gloria's sister, and her husband Dave, who are also Christians, had arrived on Monday 19th June and stayed until the Thursday and were of great support. Steve, Gloria's brother, and his wife Carol, also Christians, accepted the baton from Jackie and Dave, and everyone took me for meals at Festival Place and insisted on paying.

*On Thursday 22*nd *June*, when Jackie and Dave were going back to Southport and Steve and Carol were arriving in the afternoon, I faced a dilemma. The doctors wanted to give Gloria a tracheostomy and I was unsure whether she would have agreed to it. So, I had not slept very well the night before and in the morning went to see Rory, who was going to do the procedure. When I spoke to him he reassured me that the night before he had explained to Gloria what he proposed to do and she had not dissented. I was relieved since I did not want to do anything against Gloria's wishes. She was the medical one who knew her own mind and was very deliberate about her choices. 'You must be your own advocate when you are undergoing treatment,' she often said to me. When Gloria could not be her own advocate I would have to step up to the plate and I felt my inadequacy. I was relieved that Gloria had taken this decision herself.

Gloria had had two horrible chemotherapy sessions in the two years. Twice I went into her room and thought she was dead. There is such a thing as 'anticipated grief' and I cried myself to sleep a few times watching her suffer so much, with the added intensity of the pain in her damaged shoulder and the exceptionally large hernia she had to cope with. I've seen lots of people suffering in the thirty-four years I have been a vicar and witnessed something of the pain of my mother and father and auntie in the illnesses that led to their deaths, but this was deeper because Gloria and I were made one in marriage and what one feels, the other feels. It must be the hardest thing I have ever had to do in my life.

Gloria began to show signs of improvement. The doctors were happy with her progress but what they described as 'material' leaking from her damaged small bowel had moved so they put in a second drain. Gloria was more responsive the next day (Saturday 24th June) when Abi visited and had two hours off the ventilator. The next day I visited St Mary's once again and was greeted by Colin and Chris Barton. Gloria had three hours in the chair out of her bed. Progress was slow but there were things to be encouraged about.

On Tuesday 27th June Gloria spoke for the first time with the speaking valve in her trachy and said the immortal words, 'I want some ice cream.' Unfortunately, she could only suck water from a green foam cube on a stick. The next day she was more responsive and again had three hours off the ventilator. There was also some progress on the house sale with a cash buyer making a cheeky offer, which I declined. At least there was someone interested in buying the house, even if the offer was too low.

It was at this time that some close long-term friends began to visit. Our dear friend Joan was doing a pilgrimage of cathedrals and happened to be visiting Winchester on the Wednesday, so I drove over to the cathedral and had some tea and cake in the cathedral café. The next day (Thursday 29th June) our close friends from theological college days at Oak Hill, Nikki and Paul McVeagh, drove over from Tonbridge. They took me for a meal at Festival Place and then spent a couple of hours with Gloria and me in Critical Care. Over the weeks this would be a well-trodden path: relatives and friends picking me up at the front of Basingstoke Hospital, parking up at Eastrop Park (a beautiful spot with ornamental ponds, a fountain and a children's playground and paddling pool) and then walking the tree-lined path for about ten minutes to Festival Place, where I was treated to a variety of meals from a wide range of restaurants. This was also good for my mental health.

Nikki and Paul's visit marked three weeks of being in Basingstoke Hospital, the usual stay for a patient at the Peritoneal Malignancy Unit. It was now clear that our stay in Basingstoke Hospital was going to be much longer. It would in fact be extraordinary in so many unexpected ways. Gloria's faith and courage would shine through and show how spirituality – in particular, a Christian spirituality – enables you to overcome severe trials and as James and Paul taught, grow in perseverance and hope. We both felt the weakest as a human being but the strongest as a Christian. The power came from within.

This is not to minimise the human pain and struggle, which was intense, but our experience is that the love of Christ overcomes all setbacks, disappointments and hurts. Love like a warm blanket surrounded me from the body of Christ, expressed by family and friends who also knew the Lord Jesus as their Saviour and friend and shared this faith, hope and love. I was discovering a deeper experience of God and his living Church that was enabling me not just to cope but to flourish and to be able to reach out to others with the love of Christ.

Paul speaks of this in 2 Corinthians 1:3-4:

Praise be to the God and Father of our Lord Jesus Christ, the Father of compassion and the God of all comfort, who comforts us in all our troubles, so that we can comfort those in any trouble with the comfort we ourselves receive from God.

CHAPTER SIX

Cherished Cherub

29 June – 3 July

On Thursday 29th June, after saying goodbye to our dear friends Nikki and Paul and praying with Gloria, which I did at 7pm before leaving her each night, I did an evening drive to Carlisle, which took six hours. It was exceedingly difficult to leave Gloria, but she understood I needed to both check on the house, do necessary jobs, and bring Lizzie down to see her. I slept in until 9am the next day and it was so good to be in a normal bed. I cut the grass (which was exceptionally long) and paid the credit card bill (which was also exceptionally long!) and I took Lizzie and her husband Alan out for a meal. Steve, Gloria's brother, visited her on the Friday while I was away, and Abi visited on the Saturday. I would be back on Sunday with Lizzie. Audrey wrote on 28th June, 'Gloria is a cherished cherub, and we are proud of her.'

Going through terrible experiences can either draw you to God or push you away. Suffering is a difficult subject and as Christians we don't have all the answers but, as both James and Paul teach, if suffering is responded to by trusting in the

Lord and his mighty strength we will be able to persevere, and this will lead to building good character and character, hope, and 'hope does not disappoint us, because God has poured his Holy Spirit into our hearts' (Romans 5:5). It is possible to have joy in suffering and to suffer well as a Christian. Deep and intense pain remains, and tidal waves of grief sweep across your heart when you least expect them, but I have experienced a deeper intensity of the Lord's presence during this eighteen-week period than in my previous fifty years as a Christian. The Bible says:

> *The LORD is close to the broken-hearted and saves those who are crushed in spirit. The righteous person may have many troubles, but the LORD delivers him from them all.*
>
> (Psalm 34:18-19)

When the Bible says 'a righteous person' it means someone saved by God's grace and not by their own human merit. For instance, Ephesians 2:8-10 says:

> *For it is by grace you have been saved, through faith – and this is not from yourselves, it is the gift of God – not by works, so that no one can boast. For we are God's handiwork, created in Christ Jesus to do good works, which God prepared in advance for us to do.*

We are not saved *by* good works, but we are saved *for* good works, enabled by the grace and power of God as we grow up into maturity in Christ. Becoming a Christian over fifty years ago began a slow process of turning away from the sin of my old life and living in the power of Jesus Christ, who offers the greatest life on the planet. My life has been incredibly blessed by knowing Jesus and seeking to make him known. That begins in family relationships and then spreads out to others. Gloria became a Christian on a tough housing estate in St Helens and at once began seeing herself differently and reaching out to her family and friends. Many of her family became Christians, including her mum Joan, her sister Jackie, her brother Steve and many aunties and other relatives. Her love for Christ, who had died for her, motivated her to go to Uganda as a missionary nurse and then train as a midwife. She was known to family and friends as 'Glo' and it was that glow she had, which came from Christ living in her by the Holy Spirit, that first attracted me to her.

We brought up our two girls in the love and care of Jesus and they are both following him and are happily married. Abi and Ben are bringing up Reuben, Fred and Theo to know and love Jesus.

One of the great benefits of being a vicar is to preside at the wedding of your children. At Abi's wedding in London in 2010, I walked her in as the father of the bride and said, 'Who gives this woman to this man? That is me,' and then proceeded with leading Abi and Ben's wedding. Abi arrived with her six bridesmaids (including her sister Lizzie) on a red London bus, and we had the reception at Oak Hill College in Southgate, where I had pushed Abi around in a pushchair when I was there for training as a vicar. Lizzie got married to Alan during the pandemic in June 2021. As with Abi's wedding I walked Lizzie into church and asked, 'Who gives this woman to this man? That is me,' and then proceeded with their wedding. Because of the pandemic we could only have thirty guests, but we had a wonderful service at St John's Church, Carlisle, where I was the vicar, and a reception at Tullie House Museum and Art Gallery. Gloria, although pale and thin from the cancer, was radiant. She looks so beautiful and happy in the wedding photographs.

Just before Abi's wedding in London in 2010 Abi and Ben told me they had been at several weddings and the dad's speeches had been amazing. 'Did I have a good one prepared?' they teased. No pressure, I thought. In secret (apart from telling Lizzie who I needed to help me with the song on my phone), I decided I would sing the song 'Daughter of Mine'. Having made a preliminary speech about Abi and Ben I went ahead to try to work the phone. On the wedding photographs for the reception there are anxious faces asking, 'What is this man up to?' Eventually I managed to operate the phone to deliver the song, which was (I think) well received. Abi is the singer in the family and whilst I have sung in choirs I do not consider myself a great soloist, but Abi and Ben had set me a challenge!

At Lizzie and Alan's wedding I considered a range of ideas in total secrecy this time. Ben reckons I'm a creature of habit, so I stuck to singing another song for Lizzie, this time Stevie Wonder's 'Isn't She Lovely', written when his daughter was born, which reminded me of Lizzie's birth on New Year's Day 1986. I had progressed (not in my singing!) but in my technology since 2010, so, instead of just the song on my phone, I had a backing track and a mobile speaker. As I set out my stall in preparation for my speech and placed my mobile speaker on the reception table, both Gloria and Abi were seen to put their heads in their hands, but no one got up and left the reception as I sang my song! Afterwards, my nephew Dave, who is a lead singer in a band, suggested to his older brother Andrew, who has his own band, that I could be a contender for the lead singer they required, but I said, 'I only sing solos at my daughters' weddings, job done!' I enjoyed myself and Gloria and I were overjoyed at two daughters happily married to two Christian men. These were comforting and reassuring memories to hold on to when going through the valley of the shadow of death at Basingstoke Hospital.

On Sunday 2nd July I picked up Lizzie and we drove down to Basingstoke. It took 5 hours and 46 minutes. A good journey. Lizzie stayed in the nearby Premier Inn, and I took her into Critical Care to see her mum. In my absence, Gloria had started with terrible hallucinations from the morphine-based drugs and her protracted stay in Critical Care. I noticed that her eyes were following her nurse around the room. Pleading, she said to me, 'What are you going to do about it?' I did not know how to respond. Turning to Lizzie, she exclaimed, 'Lizzie, get on the phone to Abi and tell her to ring the police because they are trying to kill me in here!' When I tried to reassure her, she said, 'It's her, it's that one,' looking directly at her nurse. I said, 'Everyone here is trying to get you better, Gloria. They are not trying to kill you.' I apologised to the nurse, and she said, 'Don't worry, I've had this happen before, it's quite common in Critical Care.'

I spoke to Joe, one of the consultants, and he promised to try and adjust Gloria's medication to make the hallucinations not so bad, but they continued unabated for a long time.

This was one of the worst aspects for Gloria, who also saw black beetles running round the room. All three of my girls (Gloria, Lizzie and Abi) had a big fear of spiders and I was often summoned to remove them, but this was of a different order and added to Gloria's deep anguish and horror at what she imagined was happening to her. The psychologists in the hospital did offer advice, which was to make sure Gloria always had her glasses on when awake and her hearing aids in, so that she could more easily distinguish between what was real and what was imagined. One of them kindly provided a large digital clock and they also provided a whiteboard which was updated each day and said, 'Good morning, Gloria, I am your nurse today', giving the nurse's name and the date. It is hard for patients to keep their mental stability if they are lying for extended periods in a bed and in a room that never changes. The psychologists encouraged me to bring in pictures of family and friends and stick them on the whiteboard. I kept changing this so that Gloria had some variety in what she was seeing day by day, but it was exceedingly difficult for her.

At the same time, I was experiencing a mental pressure of a different sort at the hospital accommodation. I had bought a topper for my 'prison bed', which made it slightly more comfortable (my mum used to say I could sleep on a washing line!), so this was bearable but upstairs I had a very unsociable and noisy neighbour who was interrupting my sleep from around midnight to 2am on a regular basis. One of the other patient's relatives in my flat told me he was struggling with this problem. He resorted to wearing heavy duty ear defenders, but I sleep on my side, so this was not an option. The building had no sound proofing at all, which made the problem I was facing much worse. One of the nurses in Critical Care mentioned sleeping tablets but that did not appeal to me because of the side effects. Instead, I tried complaining to the admin block. They did offer to move me to another flat, but this was not suitable because it would have been at the front where there was an outdoor barbecue area, much used by staff during the warm summer weather. I would have swapped one problem for another, so I stayed where I was for now.

I produced my own plan to cope with the pattern of extreme noise from my neighbour upstairs who I nicknamed 'elephant boots'. Furniture would be dragged across the floor, there was lots of opening and closing of doors and shoes thrown on the floor, as well as lots of heavy footsteps. What was he doing? (I thought it was a man because of the heavy footsteps.) I could not speak to him because of security locks. I devised a plan that worked quite well and enabled me to get some sleep and do some work on my book. I would go to sleep at 10pm when it was quiet and set my alarm for midnight when he started banging about. Then, I would get up and work on my book until 2am when the noise subsided. After eight weeks I did try the admin block again. This time they offered me a room in the quiet block I had requested earlier when one of the nurses in Critical Care said she experienced similar problems and moved to this quieter block. This was a vast improvement on the first room, and I think the system on the ground at the admin block ought to be more sensitive and responsive to these problems, but it is a case of pressure on rooms. Management at the highest level should give priority to putting sound proofing into their accommodation blocks for the sake of their hospital staff as well as relatives of patients, but I accept doing such work would be expensive.

Again, my Christian friends came to the rescue. Our friends Nikki and Paul heard about my 'prison bed' and 'elephant boots' experience and paid for me to have three nights in the local Premier Inn. It was like being in heaven! Later, my church in Carnforth sent me a gift of £300 which was used for the same purpose. Genuine Christian love, says James, is not just about warm feelings or even fervent prayer, but involves practical action.

> *What good is it, my brothers and sisters, if someone claims to have faith but has no deeds? Can such faith save them? Suppose a brother or a sister is without clothes and daily food. If one of you says to them, 'Go in peace; keep warm and well fed,' but does nothing about their physical needs, what good is it? In the same way, faith by itself, if it is not accompanied by action, is dead.*
>
> (James 2:14-17)

This may seem to contradict what I quoted from Ephesians chapter 2 earlier about salvation being by grace alone. Martin Luther, famous for bringing this great truth back to the Church, thought that the letter of James was 'an epistle of straw', but whilst a great man he was wrong about James, who is not dealing like Paul about what saves us but with the marks of genuine faith, a changed life. Grace alone through faith alone is the root, and good works are the fruits. A genuine Christian will show something of the life of Jesus, experiencing the greatest life, in a life of service for others.

This was shown most powerfully by our late great Queen Elizabeth II, who held deep Christian convictions which she spoke about in her wonderful Christmas addresses during her many years of service. In the next chapter we will see how Paul was comforted by God in great suffering, and by the grace of God shared that comfort with others at Corinth who were suffering. This is what was happening during our eighteen weeks and a fight for life.

CHAPTER SEVEN

Much Longer and They'll Put Up a Plaque!

4 July – 2 August
Weeks Four to Eight

One of the many stars in the marvellous medical team at Basingstoke C2 is Gemma, the lead physio, who was a great motivator, great fun and consistently upbeat in difficult circumstances. It was Gemma who organised Gloria's first trip out of Critical Care in her bed, accompanied by me and Lizzie, aided by a couple of doctors and a sister, down in the lift to the ground floor and along the corridor to the garden area *on 5th July*. Gloria continued with the disturbing hallucinations of black beetles. These sorts of hallucinations are quite common in Critical Care but vary in character. Talking to other patients' relatives they were all reporting that their loved ones were seeing white mice running around the ward. I am sure Gloria would have preferred white mice to the black beetles.

On 6th July both Sue Carey and Janet Allred (our mentor Revd Frank Allred's daughters) came to see Gloria and me. These visits were a crucial support to both Gloria and me in fighting the good fight and staying positive and strong for each other.

On 10th July Gloria was back down to the garden again. She had slept very well the night before and was feeling a bit better. The garden area was a bit cold and windy, but she enjoyed some sun on her face. Later, I had coffee with Colin Barton from St Mary's at the Angel in Festival Place.

Tuesday 11th July was an important day when Gloria's trachy was taken off. Quite a moment. Sue and Paul Carey came the next day, and we had a coffee before we went in to see Gloria. Sue had come earlier on 6th July with her sister Janet. Gloria was a bit older than Sue and Janet, and became a close family friend when she became a Christian at fifteen and looked after the girls while Frank and Sheila (Frank's wife) went out. Gloria would let them stay up and then the girls would rush up to bed when their parents returned, as if they had been settled down for ages. They had many adventures together on church camps and remained close friends through the years. Their visit marked exactly five weeks in Basingstoke Hospital.

On Saturday 15th July Gloria was moved from Critical Care to the C2 recovery ward. Gloria had spent thirty-four days in Critical Care. Audrey wrote, 'Much longer and they'll put up a plaque!' Gloria was making great progress now and when she came out of Critical Care I was elated, as were all the family and friends and church fellowships who were supporting Gloria's fight for life.

On 17th July Jackie and her husband Dave took me to Festival Place. Instead of parking at Eastrop they parked in Festival Place because it was raining. They managed to lose their car in the car park, and we tried putting their details in the registration machine provided (we had never seen one of these before!) but because it was away from the CCTV cameras we had to wait for the attendant to help us. I found this very amusing until something similar happened to me a few weeks later!

On 18th July with Jackie and Dave covering I could go to Blenheim Palace for the day and see where my hero Sir Winston Churchill was born and buried. His birthplace is magnificent and the family grave a few miles away was very understated by comparison. Books about him always have many pages on his life but just a few about his death. It is interesting for me as a Christian that the gospels spend so much time on the death of Jesus, because through his sacrificial death we can have forgiveness of sins. The cross, a symbol of torture and death, was taken up by Christians as their chief symbol because of its central importance. Janet Collier, a dear friend from our time in a tough parish in Sheffield Diocese, kindly sent Gloria a small polished wooden cross, which was a great comfort as we went through eighteen weeks and a fight for life.

Gloria, as usual, was still full of fight despite the last five gruelling weeks in Critical Care. While I was at Blenheim Palace, Gemma had taken Gloria out in the wheelchair for three hours and visited Gemma's makeshift gym! It was around this time that Gloria stood unassisted for the first time. On the second time I was present, and it was hilarious. Gemma and her assistant got Gloria carefully to the edge of her bed, sitting with her feet on the base of a Zimmer frame. Gemma said, 'Right, Gloria, I will count to three and then we will assist you to stand on three.' Gemma started the countdown, but Gloria could not wait for three and went on her own on two! What a tough cookie indeed. But the hallucinations continued in C2 and were making Gloria's nights a misery. Sylvia, a senior nurse on C2, asked me to sleep for a night in Gloria's room to see if it would make a difference since she was in agony. Before I settled down for the night Sylvia suggested I go to the drinks machine and get Gloria some fizzy drink, which would give Gloria a different taste from her diet of water. Her food throughout this whole period was supplied by a food bag. All she had was a flavoured drink for all that time. Think of it!

Returning from the café area, I met a new friend as we walked down the corridor to C2. This was another patient's husband, Stephen, looking after his wife Denise. We connected at once. They had flown over from Northern Island and Stephen was staying in the Premier Inn (I was jealous!). We would be a source of great support to one another and arranged to have a meal in the restaurant next to the Premier Inn. Both Stephen and Denise were Christians.

I had brought my pyjamas and dressing gown, toothbrush, etc. and there was an en-suite in Gloria's room I could use. Sylvia made up a camp bed alongside Gloria's bed. At 11pm I went to sleep and slept soundly until 2am. When I woke up, Gloria said I had been snoring loudly and not responding to her calling my name! I was just exhausted from lack of sleep, but this was of no use to Gloria! From about 2am to 6am Gloria was in terrible anguish, tossing and turning and crying out in desperation due to the hallucinations. At 6am I had to leave since it was so upsetting to see her in such pain. I have great admiration for Sylvia and nurses like her who must cope with situations like this, sometimes for days on end. Sylvia said it was like this every night. My poor darling Gloria. I had tried to help but it did not work.

Gloria and I had now been in Basingstoke Hospital eight weeks. Because of this I became the go-to person for other relatives in the accommodation and others I met on the ward, like Stephen. I had long conversations with relatives and offered them a listening ear and tried to give them hope and encouragement. They ranged in age and sex from folk in their thirties to people of my age and older. When the time came for them to leave and go home (usually after three weeks) I would ask them to do me a favour. 'Please do two things,' I asked. 'First, read a gospel, John's gospel, with an open mind, since this is how I became a Christian fifty years ago. And second, go on YouTube and listen to Professor John Lennox, a mathematician at Oxford University and a keen Christian apologist, who has a wonderful way of explaining the Christian faith, especially issues like science and the Bible and suffering.' As I have already mentioned, helping others also helped me. Paul talks about sharing the comfort we have received from God with others in 2 Corinthians 1:3-10. In the ESV translation of the Bible it is entitled 'The God of all Comfort':

Blessed be the God and Father of our Lord Jesus Christ, the Father of mercies and God of all comfort, who comforts us in all our affliction, so that we may be able to comfort those who are in any affliction, with the comfort with which we ourselves are comforted by God. For as we share abundantly in Christ's sufferings, so through Christ we share abundantly in comfort too. If we are afflicted, it is for your comfort and salvation; and if we are comforted, it is for your comfort, which you experience when you patiently endure the same sufferings that we suffer. Our hope for you is unshaken, for we know that as you share in our sufferings, you will also share in our comfort. For we do not want you to be ignorant ... of the affliction we experienced in Asia. For we were so utterly burdened beyond our strength that we despaired of life itself. Indeed, we felt that we had received the sentence of death. But that was to make us rely not on ourselves but on God who raises the dead. He delivered us from such a deadly peril, and he will deliver us. On him we have set our hope that he will deliver us again.

Since the really encouraging news of 11th July, when Gloria's trachy was taken off, Gloria's situation had become static.

On 21st July I noted: 'An operation is not imminent but there seems a sea change today in the medical team's thinking since Gloria is static in terms of the small bowel. It has gone from the background to the foreground, I was informed.' An operation could still be a month away as she was still not strong enough. This was hard to bear but bear it we must and remain patient and hopeful. God gave me perseverance to keep on keeping on, as promised in Romans 5 and James 1.

On 2nd August, just as we reached eight weeks in hospital, we had the excellent news that a first-time buyer had made a good offer, and we accepted it gratefully. The legal process of selling our house in Carlisle began. They say selling your house is one of the most stressful things in life and it never goes smoothly. As I mentioned, there were financial pressures building but I had more important and overriding concerns: the full recovery of Gloria's health, our desired return to Morecambe for our retirement and seeing more of our three grandsons.

CHAPTER EIGHT

One Precious Bundle

16 August – 14 September
Weeks Ten to Fourteen

On Wednesday 16th August we had been ten weeks in Basingstoke Hospital. The next morning, I was over at Basing House, a ruin from the Civil War only fifteen minutes' drive from the hospital. Sylvia rang me to say that one of Gloria's lungs had collapsed while they were giving Gloria a bed bath, and they had rushed her to the nearer Critical Care B. Her condition was stable. Stephen and Denise were in the room next door to Gloria's in C2 and thought with all the commotion and blank, shocked reactions of the medical staff when they asked how Gloria was, that she had died. Patient confidentiality and privacy must be followed but I think they could have just told them she had been taken to Critical Care, but again this shows that medical staff are human and in the main do a heroic job in incredibly challenging circumstances.

I went at once to Critical Care B and was briefed by two doctors before I saw Gloria. I had been planning to go to see Abi and Ben and the grandsons for the weekend and so

I asked for guidance from Joe, one of the consultants, who thought since Yeovil was only an hour and a half away it would be okay. The medical staff had moved very quickly and had Gloria on oxygen rapidly so when they did scans there was no brain damage, for which I was very relieved, but she was still very poorly.

I had an enjoyable time in Yeovil, surrounded by a loving family, then returned to Basingstoke. Getting back on the Sunday after being with the family, with Gloria back in Critical Care A again, was the lowest point emotionally and spiritually. I suppose it was predictable after the shock of Gloria's collapse and returning from the family to the hospital again. I decided when I got back to have a meal in what would be a crowded and noisy restaurant, the Spruce Goose next to the Premier Inn, where I had made some friends among the staff. I had just parked the car and was wondering whether I had done the right thing when Cristi, our pastor at Carnforth Free Methodist, rang me for an update on Gloria's situation. It was perfect timing and immensely helpful. He prayed with me and suddenly I felt lifted and supported by the Lord and his people. Recovering my confidence, I went for a meal at the Spruce Goose. Afterwards I used the £300 my home church in Carnforth had sent me as a love gift for several nights in the Premier Inn. I had a meal with Stephen and caught up with Denise's progress, which was encouraging, and heard about Gloria's collapse from what Stephen and Denise had seen. I was so encouraged to keep going on in hope by Christian fellowship and prayer. Another church, St Margaret's near Tonbridge where our friends Nikki and Paul attended, had been praying hard and particularly a church leader called Roger had been praying and fasting for Gloria's recovery. I felt everyone at St Margaret's were in the fight with us, even though we had not met most of them. Spirituality, and specifically Christianity, which I have known personally for the fifty years since I gave my life to Christ at the age of nineteen, can bear the tremendous weight of suffering for prolonged periods and give strength and hope to the weak.

It was still extremely hard going. Our faith in God was being stress tested but we persevered, as promised in Romans 5 and James 1. This was the greatest challenge of our lives but God was faithful, and through family and friends we were given God's comfort and the grace to share that comfort with others as we saw in 2 Corinthians chapter 1. As Christians of many years we had experienced the deep love of God in Christ, and we clung on in faith. Gloria showed great courage and character in her fight for life.

Wednesday 23rd August marked eleven weeks in hospital and the next day Gloria had a second trachy put in. Very few people survive a second tracheostomy, but Gloria was a tough cookie, and she rallied. Rory told me it was okay for me to visit Portsmouth as I had planned, since it was only fifty minutes away and Gloria would be sedated and sleeping.

On Monday 4th September Jackie, Gloria's sister, and her daughter-in-law Kirsty came down from Southport to give support. They spent four days with Gloria at this critical time. It was a huge boost to Gloria and to me. Most of the time they just sat with Gloria as she slept, and Jackie read.

Wednesday 6th September marked thirteen weeks in hospital. I noted in my diary, 'Gloria off the trachy and ventilator and smiling.' Jackie and Kirsty returned to Southport the next day and again we felt things were on the up. It was still slow progress, with the drains still in place and no sign of the small bowel healing itself, but the doctors Alex and Tom, who kept this under daily review, were committed to letting Gloria's body recover itself rather than take her back into theatre, and I was very supportive of this approach.

On 14th September (her fourteenth week in Basingstoke) Gloria was transferred to C2 with the understanding that she did not need the machines in Critical Care, but she needed one-to-one nursing care, both day and night, to do everything to support Gloria's mental struggle with the hallucinations. This was implemented in C2 in her own room near the nurse's station and was vital to help Gloria have the best hope of recovery.

Audrey had written earlier on 24th August:

So sorry to hear about trachy. Gloria is going to be on ventilator for longer than the few days than we had hoped. So hard for you and the girls, never mind Gloria! She has been here before and climbed back; she has to do it again. We will be praying to that end cos Gloria is one precious bundle to the Lord, you, and us. xx

CHAPTER NINE

Gloria's Human Rock

21–24 September
Week Fifteen

So far I have not explained fully why Gloria was making such slow progress in getting better and returning home as she passionately desired, so that we could resume our retirement plans. I have said that I was told early on that the small bowel had been damaged either by a finger or an implement or by part of Gloria's body touching another part in the complex operation. I was given this information by Tom Cecil, the director of surgery, after asking him why Gloria was struggling so much after the operation. The piece of the jigsaw that completes the picture for me was provided openly by Gloria's surgeon Alex, who said that as the operation comes to an end they check meticulously to see if there are any tears and in Gloria's case they had missed the tiny tear in the small bowel, which was causing all the problems. This was his fault, he said. Alex was very transparent about all of this. My attitude, I replied, was that we are all human and mistakes happen, even with the best of intentions; it is how we respond to them that matters. The grace to respond in this Christian way clearly comes from Christ and his life within me.

One of the other relatives suggested I could sue the hospital and make lots of money. 'Why would I do that? It was a genuine mistake,' I said, 'and we all make them.' They were doing everything they could to get Gloria well and it was beginning to bear fruit. Alex's honesty and integrity in taking responsibility increased my trust in him and the strategy that he and Tom Cecil had put in place to do everything they could to aid Gloria's body to recover itself. A vital part was giving psychological support and comfort to reassure Gloria, who was still going through terrible hallucinations, and this meant one-to-one nursing care, day and night.

On 21st September, just over fifteen weeks in Basingstoke Hospital, after a week of one-to-one nursing care I was told that the daytime element was going to be withdrawn for financial reasons. I was terribly upset. I was about to go back to Carlisle to take the lease to the solicitors and empty the house ready for the exchange of contracts, which was expected imminently. In my absence, this would be the worst time to withdraw daytime nursing support for Gloria. She was not able to be her own advocate and so it was time for me to step forward. First, I spoke to Natasha, the C2 sister, and was told this was a joint decision by her and the matron and it could only be reinstated by Alex. I expressed my total opposition to this decision and asked to see Alex as soon as possible. Natasha said she would contact Alex for this to happen. In the evening, I went on the hospital trust site to register my concern.

The next day was exceedingly difficult, and I was terribly upset. Alex had been informed of my desire to see him and after a full day of clinics he came to see both me and Gloria. As he stood over her bed, Gloria said to me about Alex, 'Isn't he a lovely man,' and he replied, 'How can you say that after what I've done to you?' This was a pivotal and deeply moving moment for all three of us. In any operation and treatment there is the patient, the next of kin and the medical staff, especially the surgeon. All three are deeply involved and here we stood together. Gloria had expressed absolute trust and affection for Alex and, in characteristic fashion, Alex had acknowledged that his mistake had led to Gloria's extended suffering for fifteen weeks, with no sign of an end in sight. I said to Alex, 'Do not say that. Mistakes happen and Gloria is slowly getting better. I have seen how much good you and your fellow surgeons have done in helping many patients facing this terrible cancer to improve their chances of survival by your skill and care.'

Alex and I then went to the sister's room to meet with the nursing management to discuss the withdrawal of daytime one-to-one nursing care. I was pumped up and ready to fight Gloria's corner, but I was disarmed and delighted when Alex took the lead and first apologised that I had not been consulted and then said that he was immediately reversing the decision of the senior staff on C2. I broke down and wept with relief. Later he would tell me that this was a lack of communication between floor and management. He thought that even based on financial considerations it made more sense to keep the one-to-one daytime care since it was far more expensive for three days in Critical Care than a week of nursing care on C2. It also fitted the long-term plan of doing everything to help Gloria's body to recover by giving her the reassurance and care of one-to-one nursing to combat her hallucinations caused by the drugs and the prolonged period in Critical Care and in C2.

Alex also said later they were a victim of their own success because they do not have many Gloria's. This situation of withdrawing one-to-one daytime nursing care he agreed was a system failure, which he quickly addressed by reinstating it. Alex also told me that Natasha, the C2 sister, had accepted that the decision to withdraw daytime one-to-one nursing care was a mistake, which she regretted. Again, it is not that we make mistakes – all of us do since we are human – it is how we respond, and this was a positive response all round by the medical team.

Gloria was a tough cookie who kept bouncing back. It was three weeks since her lung collapsed in C2, and she had gone for a second time into Critical Care with ventilator and trachy and she had recovered. This is exceedingly rare. Again, she had proved what her surgeon in Newcastle had called her 'survivorship'. Things overall for Gloria were also looking much better. She still had the drains in her small bowel, which had not started to work but there were good signs. Alex was convinced that the small bowel was about to work, and this proved to be the case at seventeen weeks, which we will cover in the next chapter. The house sale was at the eight-week stage and making substantial progress towards completion in early October. I decided to drive up to Carlisle to clear the house ready for the sale. Lizzie and Alan had spent some days with Abi and family in Yeovil and were staying at Basingstoke to see Gloria from the Friday to the Monday. This was a good window of opportunity to get the house in Carlisle sold, repay the generous loan from our kind friends, stop paying bills on two homes and replenish our reserves for the future. So, on Sunday 24th September I drove up to Carlisle full of hope that Gloria was about to turn the corner, and we could soon properly settle into our Morecambe apartment and let go of the Carlisle house.

Before I left Gloria, I prayed for her, and she prayed for me, for a safe journey and success in all I needed to do in Carlisle. Again, this showed her faith and her courage and, like me, she would have said she felt the weakest as a human being, but the strongest as a Christian. Around this time Audrey referred to me as 'Gloria's human rock'. I count it a privilege to support Gloria in these years of suffering after she had supported me so faithfully for so many years. As a Ruth-like character, she was continually loyal and devoted. I was simply fulfilling my promise made at our wedding to 'have and to hold from this day forward, for better, for worse, for richer, for poorer, in sickness and in health, to love and to cherish, till death us do part, according to God's holy law'.

I would also point to Christ, who is our life and gives strength in weakness as we trust him in difficult circumstances, beyond our human power to cope. This was the experience of the apostle Paul, who is a model for the Christian life.

He [the Lord] said to me, 'My grace is sufficient for you, for my power is made perfect in weakness.' Therefore I will boast all the more gladly about my weaknesses, so that Christ's power may rest on me . . . For when I am weak, then I am strong.

(2 Corinthians 12:9-10)

Knowing Christ gives you the greatest life on the planet, with the promise and hope of eternal life. And now Christ was bringing us through the long, dark tunnel of the last two and a half years, and especially our fifteen weeks in Basingstoke. It was a very tough journey, but we could see purpose and meaning through our faith in Christ. As we persevered, God was making us more like Christ by pouring his love into our hearts by the Holy Spirit, as promised in Romans 5. The Christian faith provides rich resources of hope for suffering people to keep on keeping on through life's adversities.

CHAPTER TEN

Let's Party!

25 September – 11 October
Weeks Sixteen to Eighteen

Between the sixteenth and eighteenth week it felt like the wind was now behind us rather than in our faces, with progress on the house sale and, much more importantly, a massive breakthrough in Gloria's health. The good news on the house came first.

Exchange of contracts was pencilled in for early October with our efficient and lovely solicitor Gemma from Carlisle. She had steered us through the process to get a temporary power of attorney, which needed one signature from Gloria (since we owned the Carlisle house jointly) to give temporary attorney to Abi so she could sign on her mum's behalf. This needed to be witnessed and Paul, one of the hospital auxiliary nurses, stepped up (to my relief) to witness Gloria's weak but recognisable signature. Then Gemma rang Gloria to make sure she was willing to pass her responsibility for the house sale on to Abi, and she was happy to give her consent. In fact, Gemma commented on how much better Gloria sounded.

On Monday 25th September I travelled to Carlisle to see Gemma to finalise arrangements for the exchange of contracts. Everything was fitting into place, and we were making progress on all fronts. It was all such a relief.

I had a lot to accomplish in the week ahead and felt the pressure, but also that the Lord would answer our prayers and enable me to empty the house, take a hire van to Morecambe with things we were going to keep, drive back (it's about an hour and a half) and hand the keys of the house into the estate agents on Monday 2nd October, then drive down to Basingstoke the next day. I had previously offered twelve items free to the buyers through our solicitors. They had chosen six, including the washing machine, which I was particularly pleased and relieved about given its weight. I had not planned to have anyone else help me shift the remaining items (although I could have arranged help but thought I could manage myself). A double bed was collected on the Monday by the shop that sold it to us years previously, but I was still left with a three-seater settee, a two-seater settee, a large wooden cabinet, a fridge freezer and a tumble dryer. A local minister friend in Carlisle had given me the name of a man he knew who would take items in his trailer to the recycling for a small fee. When I contacted him on the Monday he told me his car was being mended and so he would not be available to help. What was I to do? I prayed an urgent arrow prayer, 'Lord, help me!' As a Christian of fifty years, I have seen God answer some remarkable prayers and I am a strong believer in the sovereignty of God. I was praying that God would help me in very practical ways because I was under excessive pressure and only had a few days to get a lot done but already I faced a major problem.

So, *on Tuesday 26th September* I decided to ring Carlisle Council and see if they could pick up my items. A lady answered and told me that the first available date would be 5th November! I made another quick arrow prayer to the Lord for his help to soften her heart and said, 'Can I explain my circumstances please? It may make no difference but then it just might.' She agreed and so I explained briefly about our sixteen weeks down at Basingstoke Hospital and my practical problems of emptying the house before returning on the following Tuesday. 'Give me five minutes,' she replied kindly, 'I'll see what I can do.' After a few minutes she returned with the wonderful news that our area was due for pick up on Thursday and the crew had agreed to add my collection to their list. I had to move the items down to kerbside the night before for a possible early pick up, which I was delighted to do. Afterwards I sent a thank you email to her and her colleagues, who 'had helped me beyond what they could imagine'. I did have to pay the standard small fee for the pickup, but I was so relieved and grateful to the Lord and the council for answering my prayers. On the Friday I hired a van and transported the remaining items from Carlisle to our apartment in Morecambe, returning with the van on the Monday to hand the keys of the house into the estate agent. The next day, as planned, I drove down to Basingstoke Hospital. Job done, as they say.

At seventeen weeks Gloria's bowel healed itself at last and exchange of contracts booked!

On Sunday 8th October, just before that massive turning point, Abi visited with the boys and Gloria was in good form, smiling and joking with the boys. They played with the games they had brought and the C2 staff made a big fuss of them.

From about the end of September Alex had been predicting the long-awaited breakthrough. *On 11th October*, I wrote in my diary: 'Gloria stood with assistance and Gloria's bowels started working!' There was intense joy and a palpable sense of relief from family and friends at this long-awaited news. Morecambe, here we come! The Lord had answered our prayers and the prayers of many others who were supporting us – a group who I referred to affectionately to as 'The Fellowship of the Ring'; the fellowship of the ring of prayerful family and friends who journeyed like Hobbits through the emotional roller coaster of the last two years and, in a heightened sense, the long, gruelling and grinding weeks at Basingstoke Hospital. The strategy and skill of the medics was vindicated in patiently waiting for Gloria's body to heal itself, rather than take her back into surgery with all the risks that would involve. Everywhere I went in the hospital I saw smiling faces. I felt huge relief and joy.

Everything was slotting into place after an exceptionally long wait. At the medics' meeting at C2 there was a huge cheer when the good news about Gloria's bowel beginning to work was announced by Tom Cecil. At last, we could start to make some plans. I began by booking the Ark Conference Centre, located next to the hospital but run as a separate business, for Gloria's seventieth birthday celebration on 21st November and invited family and friends and members of the local church and the medical staff. I commissioned Katie, a friend of my daughter Abi, to paint a picture entitled 'Paint a Rainbow on the Storm', from a hymn by John Newton, the former slave captain turned minister and anti-slavery campaigner, as my gift to Gloria. Katie did the commission beautifully but would not accept payment and it was gifted in the end, which was exceedingly kind of her. What a party we would have on Gloria's birthday! I began dreaming of taking Gloria home to Morecambe where everything was prepared for a happy retirement.

After two and half years of struggle and intense suffering, there was no trace of cancer. In C2 there were smiles everywhere as delighted nurses, doctors, physios, support staff, other patients and relatives rejoiced at such excellent news. Once again, Gloria stood on her own feet, this time with help from Gemma, her goal reached of being ready to go home and resume her life outside the confines of Basingstoke Hospital, which had been her home for seventeen weeks.

God had answered our prayers. Gloria, the tough cookie, had come through her long ordeal with the patient strategy of the medical team for her body to heal itself. Gloria was now eating, drinking and smiling – a lot. Exchange of contracts on the house in Carlisle was set for Friday 6th October. Everything was working as we hoped and prayed for these seventeen long and painful weeks, but now we could see the end of the long tunnel and the light ahead was very bright. The Lord had stood with us over these long and tortuous weeks. As our faith was stress tested, it was proved genuine. One of the most helpful doctrines of being what is known as a Reformed

Christian is the perseverance of the saints. God, having saved us through grace alone, and Christ alone through faith alone enables us to keep going. Romans 5 and James 1 teach us these truths about Christian perseverance in trials.

Gloria's seventieth birthday on 21st November would be a birthday to remember. After that, we should be able to go home to Morecambe. Because of her prolonged stay in a hospital bed, she might need to be in a wheelchair at first, but we would overcome that challenge as well, and I promised her that we would be walking together on the promenade, enjoying those wonderful sunsets. Everything was looking so much better. What a journey!

CHAPTER ELEVEN

Going Home

17 October

'Slow, slow progress, rapid decline.' This was a phrase Rory, one of the consultants in Critical Care had told me about, after about a month at Basingstoke Hospital. I had put it to the back of my mind because Gloria and I were determined for her to get well enough to go home to Morecambe, but it was God's plan for her to go home to heaven instead.

For a third time Gloria's lungs began to be congested, and she went for an x-ray to see how bad it was *on 13th October*. The doctor at x-ray suggested manual physio, which Gemma and her colleagues began.

On 14th October I spoke to Tom Cecil to find out how serious a development this was. Tom told me that Gloria had only just survived Critical Care with ventilator and trachy last time and would likely not survive a third. Surviving two of these challenging times in Critical Care is rare and showed Gloria's steely strength of character and her determination to get home, so we could continue our retirement together and for her to see our lovely grandson's grow up.

Tom Cecil went with me to speak to Gloria. She said, emphatically, that she did not want another time in Critical Care, she had had enough. So palliative care was arranged. This was a deep blow after her valiant fight for life over these last eighteen weeks. We all thought she would celebrate her seventieth birthday in the Ark Conference Centre and be able to return home to Morecambe, but now she was going home to Jesus.

Gloria and I often talked about heaven, now she was going to her true and lasting home, but it was devastating for all of us who loved her and desperately wanted her to remain. This outcome was not what we hoped or prayed for, but it was in the best interests of Gloria, who had fought the good fight and kept the faith, and now her reward was in sight. The hospice at Basingstoke Hospital was full so Winchester was offered but I thought it would involve too much disruption and loss of familiar and loving hospital staff in the place that became our temporary home for eighteen weeks. Eventually, it was agreed that the palliative care team (who were also lovely), with support from C2 staff, would look after Gloria on the final part of her earthly journey.

On Tuesday 17th October, at 4am, just one day short of nineteen weeks from when we had arrived at Basingstoke Hospital, Sally, one of the C2 nurses, rang to tell me to come as soon as possible and to inform the family. Sally, Sharon and Olga were holding Gloria's hands and telling her that 'Steve is coming' when Gloria went to be with her Saviour at 4.15am. Abi, Ben and I arrived shortly afterwards, followed by the rest of the family. Gloria looked so peaceful. Since

Gloria was such a tough cookie we expected a lengthy period of struggle, but because she had suffered so much and had decided 'enough was enough', she went very quickly, which was a blessing.

Shock, even though you know death is coming, is one of the most lasting experiences of grief but there was no anger, which is another common response. All ten of us relatives gathered around Gloria's bed. Somehow, I was given strength to praise God for her life and that she was now at peace with the Lord she loved and who loved her. Others joined in praise and prayer, quoting Scripture, some who do not usually pray aloud in this way. I asked Ben, my son-in-law, to read Proverbs 31 about the godly wife and we joined together in saying the Lord's Prayer.

After some time, Sally asked us to decamp to the family room at Critical Care so they could wash Gloria and put on a fresh gown. When we returned Gloria looked radiant and Sally had put the small wooden cross our friend Janet Collier had sent from the Keswick Christian Convention in July on her pillow. This was a beautiful gesture which summed up Gloria's life from the age of fifteen when she became a Christian in St Helens. Christ and his death and resurrection were central to her life. When her body left C2 for the final time, the nurses, physios and doctors lined up on either side and clapped her out. They said of her later that she was very strong and very funny.

When the family said their goodbyes in the car park the next day, I said to Kirsty, Jackie's daughter-in-law, who was not a

Christian but was clearly moved by what she had seen in her two visits with Jackie and what she had witnessed around Gloria's bed, 'Kirsty, isn't it time you became a Christian?'

'Yes,' she replied, 'I think you are right.'

Later I heard from Jackie that Kirsty had said to her mother-in-law that she wanted to be a Ruth to her Naomi. The book of Ruth is a beautiful and powerful story of godly response to grief about a young woman and her mother-in-law Naomi. This comment by Kirsty was so encouraging because, as I said in chapter 1, Gloria was a Ruth character who had given me a new Bible at our engagement in 1983 with these words of Ruth to her mother-in-law:

> *Where you go I will go, and where you stay I will stay. Your people will be my people and your God my God. Where you die I will die, and there I will be buried. May the LORD deal with me, be it ever so severely, if even death separates you and me.*
>
> (Ruth 1:16-17)

Life is hard and short, and Gloria's sudden death was a bitter blow so soon after she had overcome her problems and typically was standing on her feet at week seventeen, but the Lord gives strength to the weak and the broken-hearted. At the same time, I heard from our solicitors that the couple who were buying our house had gone to Vietnam for a family event and would only return six weeks later. My deep conviction is that our days are in God's hands but why, after eighteen weeks of a valiant fight for life, had the Lord taken Gloria to heaven? Why had he not taken her during the operation, if this was to be the outcome? Why had he not taken her, as I thought on two occasions, during two years of brutal chemotherapy? What was the purpose of all this extended and intense suffering for it to end in Gloria's death, just a few weeks short of her seventieth birthday? Where was God and the transforming hope we see in Romans 5 and James 1? These questions weighed heavily on my heart.

CHAPTER TWELVE

Into the Ark

18 October

The day after Gloria died I made my way to the Ark Conference Centre, which had become my watering hole and place of comfort during the eighteen weeks and a fight for life, where the staff were amazingly friendly and the food incredibly good. The ark in the Bible (Genesis 6:11-21) for me stands metaphorically for God's people, the Church, and the sea the spirit of the world, so this is another reason this was my 'happy place' at Basingstoke Hospital.

Two unexpected events raised my shocked and despairing spirit.

On the way to ring the funeral directors and meet up with the family at the Ark, I was comforted in my sorrow by an unusual sight just outside the building. Two African medics, a man and a woman, were walking towards me. Suddenly, the woman, with joy written all over her beautiful face, was leaping into the air and twirling around like a ballerina. This was remarkable since she was not built like one, but she was clearly so happy about something that she had to express it in this wonderful way. I had the most comforting thought as I remembered what Jackie had told me about Gloria drawing a ballerina between wallpapering in their council house bedroom in St Helens. 'This,' I said to myself in pure joy, 'is what Gloria is doing now in heaven with Jesus. She is out of pain and enjoying her reward.' Just as the paralysed man healed by the power of Jesus through Peter and John went 'walking and leaping and praising God' (Acts 3:8 ESV), so Gloria was doing the same in heaven. When I arrived at the Ark Conference Centre the staff were terribly upset and incredibly supportive after I told them about Gloria, and I sat down in the foyer and prepared to ring the funeral directors recommended by Colin Barton, the church warden at St Mary's, Basingstoke.

As I paused to control myself, one of the three consultant surgeons, who I had seen with Alex and Tom but never spoken to, approached me. He said, 'I am Andrew Samuels, one of the consultants. I wanted to say I have had many conversations with Gloria, and she was a lovely person. I am praying for you at this difficult time.'

'Are you a Christian?' I asked.

'Yes, I am,' he said and told me where he worshipped in Basingstoke, at one of the other Anglican churches.

These two experiences were so comforting and gave me strength to make the difficult call to the funeral directors. I made an appointment to meet the funeral director the following Tuesday, 24th October, and on the same day register

Gloria's death at Basingstoke Registry. Then I drove up to Morecambe and the next day went to Lancaster Crematorium to arrange Gloria's scattering of ashes in the woodland area, after the funeral at St Mary's and her cremation at Basingstoke Crematorium, which we arranged for Monday 30th October. I brought down from Morecambe, at Abi's suggestion, the clothes Gloria had worn at Lizzie's wedding, which Gloria would be cremated in. This seemed so fitting since she had been incredibly happy on that day and looked radiant. I also arranged a celebration service for Gloria's life at our home church in Carnforth for her birthday on Tuesday 21st November. I asked Paul and Nikki McVeagh, our good friends from theological college who lived in Tonbridge, to lead the funeral service at St Mary's, and Cristi Murgu, our Romanian pastor, to lead the celebration of Gloria's life at Carnforth Free Methodist with Graham Stamford (who I worked for in local schools' ministry in Lancaster and Morecambe 1981–1986) to preach a sermon.

It seemed proper to have Gloria's funeral at St Mary's since it had become my temporary spiritual home and it was nearer for Abi, Ben and boys, Steve, Carol, Nikki and Paul to get to and other kind friends like Sue and Paul Carey. The celebration service and scattering of ashes would be in the Lancaster area, nearer for Lizzie, Alan, Jackie, Dave, Kirsty and friends from our time in Lancaster forty years before when we met and married. This also enabled other family members and new friends from our apartment block in Morecambe and elsewhere in the area to come along and hear about Gloria's life, a life well lived. Paul McVeagh had arranged to meet us all on Zoom to discuss the funeral and celebration arrangements and everyone was happy with my suggestions.

What about all the questions we had when Gloria unexpectedly died, after two and a half years of a fight for life? What had been the purpose of all that suffering? Two insights have been extremely helpful. One given to me soon after Gloria's death and the other a year later when reading an updated copy of John Piper's *Desiring God*, which includes a chapter on suffering. My daughter Abi sent me an insightful quotation from George Muller (1805–1898),[6] who was a Christian evangelist who set up orphanages and schools. He established 117 schools that gave Christian education to more than 120,000 children. He never asked for money yet raised £100,000 to build the schools. He also cared for 10,000 orphans. When his beloved wife Mary died, he wrote these moving words.

Beloved brethren and sisters in Christ, I ask you to join with me in hearty praise and thanksgiving to my precious Lord for his lovingkindness in having taken my darling, beloved wife out of the pain and suffering she has endured, into his presence; and as I rejoice in everything for her happiness, so I now rejoice as I realise how far happier she is, in beholding her Lord who she loved so well, than in any joy she has known or could know here. I ask you also to pray that the Lord will so enable me to have fellowship in her joy that my bereaved heart may be occupied with her blessedness instead of my unspeakable loss.

6. https://en.wikipedia.org/wiki/George_M%C3%BCller

George Muller clearly had an incredibly good marriage with his wife Mary and was heartbroken when she died. He asked no questions about her suffering (which appears protracted) but focuses on the goodness of God and her joy and blessedness of being with the Lord she loved, instead of his unspeakable loss. His long walk with Jesus had shaped his heart and mind to think of 'the hope of the glory of God,' as Paul outlines in Romans 5:5, which is the chief end of man and to enjoy him forever. This is what Mary is now enjoying. Her earthly fight was at an end and now she had obtained her goal. This should be the focus of George Muller's heart and mind, and I began to realise it should also be my focus. This eternal perspective is the message of hope of the whole Bible. We are not meant to see Christianity as a means to a good life here on earth, but a God-ward life, focused on the new heaven and earth to come.

This is shown by Paul's joy in suffering expressed in Romans 5:2-4 (ESV):

Through him we have also obtained access by faith into this grace in which we stand, and we rejoice in hope of the glory of God. Not only that, we rejoice in our sufferings, knowing that suffering produces endurance, and endurance produces character, and character produces hope.

Rejoicing in the hope of the glory of God (the purpose for which we were made) leads to rejoicing in suffering, as part of God's means of shaping our Christian character. Piper's principle, in his book *Desiring God*, says, 'God is most glorified in me, when I am most satisfied in him.'[7]

---

7. Piper, *Desiring God, p. 2.*

The second insight for me came much later, in fact during the first anniversary of Gloria's death as I completed this memoir. Piper writes:

All experiences of suffering in the path of Christian obedience, whether from persecution, sickness or accident have this in common: They all threaten our faith in the goodness of God and tempt us to leave the path of obedience. Therefore, every triumph of faith and all perseverance in obedience are testimony to the goodness of God and the preciousness of Christ – whether the enemy is sickness, Satan, sin, or sabotage.[8]

Fifty years of being a Christian, thirty-nine years of marriage to Gloria and forty years of Christian ministry have taught my heart the absolute goodness of God towards his children. The cross of Jesus is the ultimate proof of the goodness of God and Paul clinches the argument for me in Romans 8:32 (ESV):

He who did not spare his own Son but gave him up for us all, how will he not also with him graciously give us all things?

Piper concludes his chapter on suffering in his book *Desiring God* with what he calls 'the essence of Christian Hedonism':

In the pursuit of joy through suffering, we magnify the all-satisfying worth of the Source of our joy. God himself shines as the brightness at the end of our tunnel of pain. If we do not communicate that he is the goal and ground of our joy in suffering, then the very meaning of our

---

8.   Ibid p. 257.

suffering will be lost. The meaning is this: God is gain. God is gain. God is gain.

The chief end of man is to glorify God. And it is truer in suffering than anywhere else that God is most glorified in us when we are most satisfied in him. My prayer, therefore, is that the Holy Spirit would pour out on his people around the world a passion for the supremacy of God in all things. And I pray that he would make plain that the pursuit of joy in God, whatever the pain, is a powerful testimony to God's supreme and all satisfying worth.[9]

I hope, dear reader, that you have a fresh and helpful perspective on suffering. The Christian faith gives wonderful hope, based on the goodness of God.

---

9. Ibid p. 257.

CHAPTER THIRTEEN

Into the Church

St Mary's, Basingstoke
30 October

This is the poem Reuben, our eldest grandson (then aged ten), wrote for his grannie's funeral and after the opening hymn he was the first to stand up. He read it beautifully and his grannie would have been so proud of him.

My grannie was the best.
My family was always her favourite guest,
She used to give me lots of snacks,
The chocolate she had was in stacks,
She was so great.
When we drove to her house we were always late,
So, we got excited when we saw Grannie,
The fun we have is uncountable on a tally,
We used to muck about together,
She will always be in my heart forever.

Paul McVeagh led the service with great tact and warmth focusing on Gloria as a faithful wife, mother and grandmother, who had fulfilled that promise she made in 1983 when she gave me the new Bible with the words of Ruth to Naomi:

Where you go I will go, and where you stay I will stay. Your people will be my people and your God my God. Where you die I will die, and there I will be buried. May the LORD deal with me, be it ever so severely, if even death separates you and me.

(Ruth 1:16-17)

That loyalty by Ruth to Naomi and her God was expressed by Gloria over all the years of our long and fruitful marriage of thirty-nine years.

I said to Paul that I wanted to share something from the front about Gloria but was not sure if I could do it. So I gave him a copy of what I intended to say, so he could read it if I faltered. I would signal him yes or no on the last hymn. When he caught my eye in the last hymn I signalled that I would do it and at once felt I did not have the strength. This has been typical of our eighteen weeks and a fight for life, when I felt the weakest as a human being and the strongest as a Christian. Just as I stepped forward to the podium I felt strength in weakness from the Lord, and this is what I said:

A Tribute to a Noble Wife

First, thanks to Paul and Nikki for leading us in our purpose to bring glory to the Lord who was the Source of Gloria's character, her strength in adversity and her good humour.

Thanks to the away team – some have travelled a long way to be here.

Thanks to the home team, especially Critical Care and C2, which in our eighteen weeks in Basingstoke became home, and to St Mary's, Basingstoke, who have been a spiritual second home to me.

Gloria was the love of my life. She was my best friend, my best critic, and my biggest fan. I often said to her she was a better Christian than me and would be nearer the throne in heaven, but she would not have it. Some of my last words to her were, 'We will meet again in glory.'

Thanks most of all to the Lord who brought Gloria and me together thirty-nine years ago in Christian marriage, with two wonderful daughters, Lizzie and Abi, married to two wonderful men, Alan and Ben. Gloria and I are so proud of our grandsons, Reuben, Fred and Theo. Our whole family are trying to follow Christ the best we can. I thank God for our wider family, especially Jackie and Dave and Steve and Carol and many good friends.

I called Gloria my Proverbs 31 wife. At the end of a section describing a wife of noble character it ends, 'Many women do noble things, but you surpass them all. Charm is deceptive and beauty fleeting but a woman who fears the Lord is to be praised.'

Gloria had demonstrated 'joy in suffering', the joy Paul and James describe, motivated by her Christian faith since giving her life to Jesus aged fifteen. The Source of her joy was

God himself. As John Piper says, 'God himself shines as the brightness at the end of our tunnel of pain . . . The meaning [of pain] is this: God is gain. God is gain. God is gain.'[10]

That is why Paul wrote these words:

For I consider that the sufferings of this present time are not worth comparing with the glory that is to be revealed to us . . . No, in all these things we are more than conquerors through him who loved us. For I am sure that neither death nor life, nor angels nor rulers, nor things present nor things to come, nor powers, nor height nor depth, nor anything else in all creation, will be able to separate us from the love of God in Christ Jesus our Lord.

(Romans 8:18, 37-39 ESV)

Audrey and Don Andrew sent a letter on 22nd October with these sentiments:

We have known Gloria since she was a teenager right through to her Granny years. Years walking with the Lord and being a witness for Him. Although there have been occasional sad times, there has been lots of laughter and 'leg pull' in our friendship. We have many happy memories to look back on which make us smile.

Whilst Gloria's funeral was a day of sadness, it was also the joy of a life well lived.

---

10. Piper, *Desiring God*, p. 257.

CHAPTER FOURTEEN

Into the Future

21 November

On 21st November 2023, Gloria's birthday, the family gathered in the morning at Lancaster Crematorium for the scattering of Gloria's ashes in the woodland area, and then went for a meal together in Carnforth, followed by the celebration service at Carnforth Free Methodist. As well as the family I invited Joan and Brian, who live just five minutes from my apartment and in whose house in Lancaster Gloria and I had met over forty years previously. Joan had sung at our wedding and Brian had played the organ. I led us in a short service and word from the Bible. When Gloria's ashes were poured out in the shape of a cross, by a Silver Birch, Joan and Brian led us spontaneously and beautifully in the hymn 'The Old Rugged Cross'. It was a special moment. As we walked away, Gloria's sister Jackie said, 'Dave, that's the sort of service I want when my time comes.' When my own time comes, my ashes will be poured in the same place as Gloria's by the Silver Birch, unless the Lord returns before my death.

Because Gloria died in hospital on 17th October 2023 it appears her fight for life was lost, but this was not the case. Her fight was the fight of faith, and she fought that fight all through her Christian life, right to the end of her pilgrimage on earth. Sue and Paul Carey wrote a card for me shortly after Gloria's death. It was written freehand quoting lots of Scripture promises and included this:

> *All the days ordained for each of us were written in his book before one of them came to be – and so Gloria's is not a life cut short but a life wonderfully <u>complete</u>. Stay in touch. As the Lord's people, as brothers and sisters in Christ, we are with you all the way home.*

I will keep on with the Christian life, the greatest life on the planet, until the Lord calls me home. I have some marvellous Christian family and friends for the journey to heaven.

For Christians death is not the end but a wonderful and perfect new life without suffering or death. Gloria and I will meet again in heaven and be in the Lord's presence for ever. We will not be married (Jesus taught there will be no marriage in heaven), but Gloria and I will be roommates. The depth and beauty of our relationship on earth will be surpassed in heaven, and everyone who trusts in Christ for salvation will share in the blessings of a new heaven and earth.

Pete Jackson, the present vicar of our first parish, St Andrew's, Kendray, Barnsley, has just invited me to visit and preach. It was twenty-five years ago that Gloria and I left Barnsley after eight years setting up a new parish and a new building. My sermon will conclude a series on 'Waiting' and be entitled

'The wait will be worth it', on the text of Revelation 21, which begins:

Then I saw a new heaven and a new earth, for the first heaven and the first earth had passed away, and the sea was no more. And I saw the holy city, new Jerusalem, coming down out of heaven from God, prepared as a bride adorned for her husband. And I heard a loud voice from the throne saying, 'Behold, the dwelling place of God is with man. He will dwell with them, and they will be his people, and God himself will be with them as their God. He will wipe away every tear from their eyes, and death shall be no more, neither shall there be mourning, nor crying, nor pain anymore, for the former things have passed away.'

(Revelation 21:1-4)

So, Gloria's eighteen-week fight for life was not in vain. Her life and faith and good humour and courage came from her trust in Christ and the way he worked his purposes through her life of struggles and joys. This touched many at Basingstoke, as well as bringing our family and friends together as never before in a fellowship of suffering and joy. The challenge now is to keep that closer relationship with the Lord and with one another alive and growing. My personal situation has dramatically changed, and I must embrace this new life without Gloria. My purpose is still the same: to know Christ and make him known. To enjoy that greatest life that Jesus promised in John 10:10, 'I have come that they may have life, and have it to the full.' This is Christ living in and through believers, confident that 'any bush' will do as his power flows through us as we submit to his loving rule. Jesus says in John 15:5:

I am the vine; you are the branches. If you remain in me and I in you, you will bear much fruit; apart from me you can do nothing.

God is using me to speak of this greatest life and he is opening exciting opportunities near and far. I have six local church fellowships who are regularly inviting me to speak. In May 2023 I returned to Basingstoke for a thank you tour, where I stayed with my kind friends Colin and Chris Barton. I went into the hospital to meet the doctors and nurses to thank them for what they did for Gloria and me and to ask them if they would like to collaborate on the writing of this book. Both Alex and Tom were very enthusiastic, and I had a wonderful time with the staff on C2. It was a remarkable day. My heart is filled with a joy beyond human understanding because I know Gloria is out of pain and in the presence of Jesus, enjoying her reward and dancing like a ballerina. Grief and pain remain, but I have great comfort from the truths I have known for fifty years that were tested and proved in the fires of eighteen weeks and a fight for life, resulting in a rock-solid hope that cannot be destroyed, as described in Romans 5 and James Chapter 1.

Conclusion

I have said how much the story of Ruth resonates with our family. The Ruth connection is carried on in the middle name of Abi and Ben's second son and our second grandson, Freddie Boaz. Hebrew society was structured by God's law to look after widows and maintain family names through the system of 'kinsman redeemers' (see Leviticus 25). If an Israelite descended into poverty their nearest kinsman had the responsibility to step in and pay the redemption price. There was also an obligation to marry the widow to make sure the man's name and estate continued. Boaz is good and kind and steps in not only to help Naomi, but also to marry Ruth. They have a son called Obed, who is the grandfather of David and the forefather of Jesus. In the New Testament we see Jesus as our kinsman redeemer who steps in to redeem us. Hebrews 2:11 says:

Both the one who makes people holy and those who are made holy are of the same family. So Jesus is not ashamed to call them brothers and sisters.

Naomi, Ruth's mother-in-law, experiences terrible loss and tells her friends not to call her Naomi, which means pleasant, and instead Mara, which means bitter (see Ruth 1:20). It is tempting to feel bitter when severe suffering comes. Through the help of her daughter-in-law Ruth and the providential intervention of Boaz, Naomi's sadness is turned into joy, since the story ends with baby Obed on Naomi's lap. A new life of great blessing beckons. She can be, by God's grace, better not bitter.

Like Naomi I am experiencing new life and fresh touches of God's grace, while my heart aches for heaven. I am better not bitter. This story, *Eighteen Weeks and A Fight for Life*, has shown how spirituality, and specifically Christianity, can transform our suffering and bring much blessing and hope. Whether you are a person of faith or none I hope our story will draw you to the kinsman redeemer Christ and experience through his life and presence, strength in weakness and the greatest life on the planet. Life on earth is tough for the Christian, but because of the resurrection of Christ we have the promise of heaven. This Christian hope sustained Gloria and me through our suffering and it will sustain you, if you put your faith in the living Christ who has paid the price for our sins and rose again to live his life in and through us. He gives us his resurrection power to live for him on earth and he promises heaven for all who turn in faith to him. The great American evangelist Dwight L. Moody (1837–1899) famously said, 'Heaven is a prepared place for a prepared people!'[11]

11. https://en.wikipedia.org/wiki/Dwight_L._Moody

Gloria, at the end of her eighteen weeks and a fight for life, echoing the apostle Paul's last words in 2 Timothy 4:7-8, could say,

> *I have fought the good fight, I have finished the race, I have kept the faith. Now there is in store for me the crown of righteousness, which the Lord, the righteous Judge, will award to me on that day – and not only to me, but also to all who have longed for his appearing.*

On the day of her death these verses were applied to Gloria by a member of her family as we gathered around her bed in praise and worship of the Lord. From her conversion aged fifteen to when she ended her earthly pilgrimage aged sixty-nine, Gloria was a prepared person for a prepared place.

For myself, I would echo the prayer request of George Muller, quoted in Chapter 12:

> *Pray that the Lord will so enable me to have fellowship in [Gloria's] joy that my bereaved heart may be occupied with her blessedness instead of my unspeakable loss.*

Appendix

1. How Help from America enabled Basingstoke Hospital to be the leading unit in Europe.

I asked Alex, Gloria's surgeon at Basingstoke, how the relationship with America came about and how it helps them to keep improving in their treatment. This is his reply:

> In regard to our connection to the US, it all started when Brendan Moran had a patient who presented with Pseudomyxoma peritonei back in the 1990s. Prof. Bill Heald (world famous surgeon who changed the way we operated for rectal cancer) had heard of Dr Paul Sugarbaker in Washington DC who had pioneered CRS and HIPEC. He was then asked if he was willing to travel to the UK to operate together on the patient. They did the operation and then Brendan Moran did another patient (from Scotland) and then another one and by the early 2000s Basingstoke was commissioned to provide

CRS and HIPEC for Pseudomyxoma initially followed by colorectal peritoneal metastasis in 2012. My colleague Faheez Mohamed did his research (MD) with Paul Sugarbaker back in the early 2000s before going to Basingstoke in 2009.

We as a group have maintained very close relationship with Dr Sugarbaker and he has visited many times to Basingstoke since his first visit back in the 1990s. We also have links with several centres in the US and have collaborated in research projects with these centres too.

Alexios Tzivanakis
Consultant Surgeon, Peritoneal Malignancy Institute, Basingstoke

2. Data suggesting a link between spirituality and improved outcomes in medicine.

Numerous examples could be provided, here are just three: two from The American National Library of Medicine and an article from *The Lancet Regional Health – Europe* entitled, 'Time to integrate spiritual needs in health care'.

Example one: Religious attendance and cause of death over 31 years[12]

Doug Oman, John H. Kurata, William J. Strawbridge, Richard D. Cohen

---

12. https://pubmed.ncbi.nlm.nih.gov/12075917/

Abstract

Objective: Frequent attendance at religious services has been reported by several studies to be independently associated with lower all-cause mortality. The present study aimed to clarify relationships between religious attendance and mortality by examining how associations of religious attendance with several specific causes of death may be explained by demographics, socioeconomic status, health status, health behaviours, and social connections.

Method: Associations between frequent religious attendance and major types of cause-specific mortality between 1965 and 1996 were examined for 6,545 residents of Alameda County, California. Sequential proportional hazards regressions were used to study survival time until mortality from circulatory, cancer, digestive, respiratory, or external causes.

Results: After adjusting for age and sex, infrequent (never or less than weekly) attenders had significantly higher rates of circulatory, cancer, digestive, and respiratory mortality (p < 0.05), but not mortality due to external causes. Differences in cancer mortality were explained by prior health status. Associations with other outcomes were weakened but not eliminated by including health behaviours and prior health status. In fully adjusted models, infrequent attenders had significantly or marginally significantly higher rates of death from circulatory (relative hazard [RH] = 1.21, 95 percent confidence interval [CI] = 1.02 to 1.45), digestive (RH = 1.99, p < 0.10, 95 percent CI = 0.98 to 4.03), and respiratory (RH = 1.66, p < 0.10, 95 percent CI = 0.92 to 3.02) mortality.

Conclusions: These results are consistent with the view that religious involvement, like high socioeconomic status, is a general protective factor that promotes health through a variety of causal pathways. Further study is needed to determine whether the independent effects of religion are mediated by psychological states or other unknown factors.

Example two: Does religious attendance prolong survival? A six-year follow-up study of 3,968 older adults[13]

H.G. Koenig, J.C. Hays, D.B. Larson, L.K. George, H.J. Cohen, M.E. McCullough, K.G. Meador, D.G. Blazer

Abstract

Methods: A probability sample of 3,968 community-dwelling adults aged 64-101 years residing in the Piedmont of North Carolina was surveyed in 1986 as part of the Established Populations for the Epidemiologic Studies of the Elderly (EPESE) programme of the National Institutes of Health. Attendance at religious services and a wide variety of sociodemographic and health variables were assessed at baseline. Vital status of members

---

13. https://pubmed.ncbi.nlm.nih.gov/10462170/

was then determined prospectively over the next 6 years (1986–1992). Time (days) to death or censoring in days was analysed using a Cox proportional hazards regression model.

Results: During a median 6.3-year follow-up period, 1,777 subjects (29.7%) died. Of the subjects who attended religious services once a week or more in 1986 (frequent attenders), 22.9% died compared to 37.4% of those attending services less than once a week (infrequent attenders). The relative hazard (RH) of dying for frequent attenders was 46% less than for infrequent attenders (RH: 0.54, 95% CI 0.48-.0.61), an effect that was strongest in women (RH 0.51, CI 0.434-.59) but also present in men (RH 0.63, 95% CI 0.52-0.75). When demographics, health conditions, social connections, and health practices were controlled, this effect remained significant for the entire sample (RH 0.72, 95% CI 0.64-.81), and for both women (RH 0.65, 95% CI 0.554-.76, p<.0001) and men (RH 0.83, 95% CI 0.69-1.00, p=.05).

Conclusions: Older adults, particularly women, who attend religious services at least once a week appear to have a survival advantage over those attending services less frequently.

Disclaimer by the American National Library of Medicine

This disclaimer relates to PubMed, PubMed Central (PMC), and Bookshelf. These three resources are scientific literature databases offered to the public by the U.S. National Library of Medicine (NLM). NLM is not a publisher, but rather collects, indexes and archives scientific literature published by other organisations. The presence of any article, book or document in these databases does not imply an endorsement of, or concurrence with, the contents by NLM, the National Institutes of Health (NIH), or the U.S. Federal Government.

Example three: *The Lancet*, 'Time to integrate spiritual needs in health care'[14]

Editorial Volume 28 May 2023

Over the past decades there has been a growth in the field of spirituality and health research showing a positive influence of spirituality and spiritual care, on both mental and physical health outcomes. Providing spiritual care to patients with serious illness has been associated with better end-of-life outcomes, and unmet spiritual needs can be associated with poorer patient quality of life and wellbeing. As per literature estimates, spirituality is important to most patients with serious illness (71-99%) and spiritual care is frequently desired by patients with serious illness (50-96%). Despite these findings, spiritual needs of patients with serious illness are frequently unaddressed within medical care – estimates of patients not receiving spiritual care range from 49 to 91%.

---

14. https://www.thelancet.com/journals/lanepe/article/PIIS2666-7762(23)00067-4/fulltext

DR JAMES GREEN

HOW TO
TALK
TO YOUR
PET

...AND
OTHER
ANIMALS

To Noah, Wilbur, Finn and Oliver –
with your wonderful curiosity for all
animals, this one's for you.

First published in Great Britain in 2025 by Wren & Rook

ISBN: 978 1 5263 6639 9

1 3 5 7 9 10 8 6 4 2

MIX
Paper | Supporting
responsible forestry
FSC® C104740

FSC
www.fsc.org

Wren & Rook
An imprint of
Hachette Children's Group
Part of Hodder & Stoughton Limited
Carmelite House
50 Victoria Embankment
London EC4Y 0DZ

The authorised representative in the EEA is Hachette Ireland, 8 Castlecourt Centre,
Castleknock Road, Castleknock, Dublin 15, D15 XTP3, Ireland. (email: info@hbgi.ie)

An Hachette UK Company
www.hachette.co.uk
www.hachettechildrens.co.uk

Printed and bound in Great Britain by Clays Ltd, Elcograf S.p.A.

FROM TV VET
DR JAMES GREENWOOD

HOW TO

TALK
TO YOUR
PET

... AND
OTHER
ANIMALS

wren
&rook

ILLUSTRATED BY JACK VIANT

CONTENTS

Hello, I'm Dr James, and I absolutely LOVE animals.

I'm lucky enough to have always been surrounded by amazing pets. From dogs, sheep, horses and rabbits to fish, crabs, frogs and even fire-bellied newts. (DON'T WORRY, THAT JUST MEANS THEY HAVE ORANGE BELLIES – THEY'RE NOT REALLY ON FIRE!)

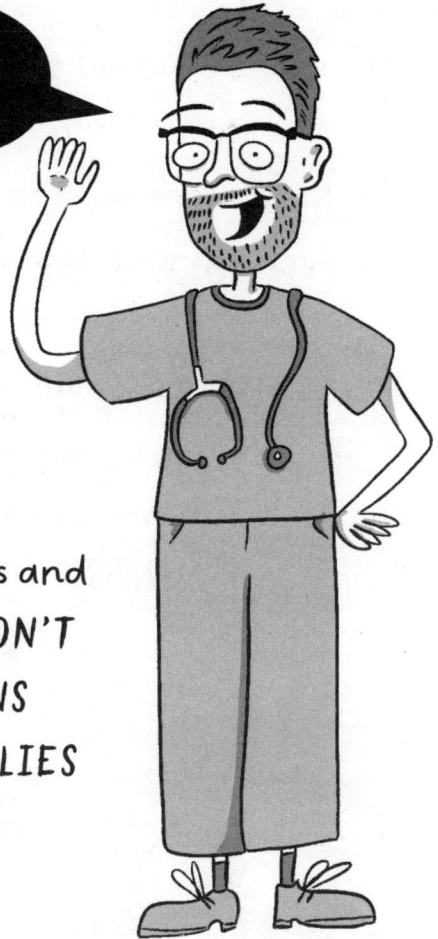

When I was growing up, I always dreamt of being a vet so that I could help my pets when they got sick – and one day MY DREAM CAME TRUE!

I have travelled the world helping animals and learnt LOADS along the way. That's what made me want to write the book you're holding right now.

I want to show you what your pets are trying to say to you, how you can tell if they FEEL HAPPY and what's really going on INSIDE THEIR MINDS.

I have a rescue dog called DOLLY who lives with me now and travels everywhere I go. In a way, Dolly has helped me write this book as I have learnt SO MUCH from her.

You'll find her **CUTE LITTLE NOSE** popping up from time to time with some top tips and helpful hints. Make sure you stop and give her a little tickle under the chin when you see her, though – **SHE LOVES THE ATTENTION!**

Our pets can speak, but only to those who know how to *LISTEN*. Whether they're a dog or a cat, a hamster or a horse, there are things that are helpful to know which apply to most pets.

SPEECH: Most animals will appreciate you talking to them in a quiet voice, using CALM, KIND TONES and GENTLE WORDS.

FOOD: Food can be used as a REWARD as well as a daily ESSENTIAL, and it's a great tool to help BUILD A BOND with our pets.

FOOD

BODY LANGUAGE: We need to be aware of how our own bodies move in front of our pets. Our actions can give REALLY STRONG MESSAGES to our pets, so try to use CALM, SLOW MOVEMENTS around animals and always make sure they know where you are.

9

TOUCH: Most pets ENJOY PHYSICAL CONTACT with their owners (except tarantulas . . . oh, and fish!). There are certain areas where our pets enjoy being stroked and certain areas where they really dislike being touched (MORE ON THAT LATER!).

RESPECTING THEIR CHOICE:

One of the best ways we can talk to our pets is through LISTENING and OBSERVING what THEY want to do. Having a pet is not about making them do what we want them to do – IT'S A TWO-WAY FRIENDSHIP!

So, on that note, I think it's time we start talking to some animals! We're kicking things off with everyone's best friend – DOGS!

10

Humans started living with dogs thousands of years ago, in the middle of the last Ice Age. Although they weren't quite 'dogs' as we know them today – they were actually WOLVES!

It's believed that as humans' and wolves' territories overlapped, they became more and more used to seeing each other. Eventually, it's thought that wolves would eat food scraps

humans left behind and would seek warmth by their fires. Aw!

Before long, they were firm friends, and the wolves slowly evolved into the dogs we love today, from TEENY TINY CHIHUAHUAS to MA-HOOO-SIVE GREAT DANES. And they were happily communicating with each other too! BUT HOW?

SMELL

Dogs want to sniff EVERYTHING, from lamp-posts to each other's bottoms (HOW RUDE!). They also want to smell US! That way, they can tell if we have met other dogs that day or what we had for breakfast. Some dogs can even smell when we are poorly through changes in how our sweat smells!

Letting dogs sniff us is like humans giving each other a handshake or a hug. It's a dog's way of saying:

HELLO, HOW'S YOUR DAY GOING?

This is why it's important to always allow dogs to sniff you when they first meet you. Keep your hands by your side with your palms facing your legs, and allow the dog to come to you and sniff the back of your hand. This shows the dog you are their friend and you have *GOOD DOGGY MANNERS!*

HOWEVER, IT'S IMPORTANT NEVER TO PUT YOUR FIST IN FRONT OF A DOG'S NOSE FOR THEM TO SNIFF AS YOU MAY ACCIDENTALLY SCARE THEM.

THE PET FILES

Have you ever wondered why a dog's nose is wet? It is to help 'trap' all the different scent particles in the air so they never miss a new smell! This is also why they lick their noses – to give their super-smelling snouts a quick refresh before even more smells come along.

EYE CONTACT

One key way we can talk with dogs is through EYE CONTACT. For instance, when Dolly sees me go towards her treat jar, she looks directly into my eyes. She knows I'm a big softie and might end up giving her a treat! Other than monkeys (WHICH ARE DEFINITELY NOT PETS!), dogs are the only species that will choose to use eye contact to 'TALK' to us.

Some dogs will even look left or right when you move your eyes, to see what you are looking at, or they may even walk off in that direction to go and investigate. Making short amounts of soft eye contact with dogs is one way of talking directly with them and their way of talking back. It helps us FORM BONDS with them and tells them they are a part of the family.

IMPORTANT NOTE: If a dog makes short bursts of kind eye contact, it is a positive sign that they feel comfortable. However, a long stare with big, wide-open eyes and no blinking is a sign that the dog is feeling threatened and should be left alone. Never stare directly into a dog's eyes for a long time – this is very scary for them.

AMAZING EARS

Sounds that might not be that scary for us can be *TERRIFYING FOR DOGS* – like the vacuum cleaner, loud bangs from fireworks or rumbling thunder overhead (*OK, THAT CAN SOMETIMES BE A BIT SCARY FOR US TOO!*).

IT'S TOO LOUD!

To help them out, we should avoid making any loud, sudden noises around them.

Making quiet, calm sounds, though, can be very comforting.

17

Talking to our dogs is a great way to help them *BUILD TRUST* and recognise who we are.

Some studies show dogs can remember up to *250 DIFFERENT WORDS!* A good way to practise talking with your dog is to always use kind words and phrases. They can't understand the words, but the way we say them is what counts.

Words like I'M REALLY HAPPY TO SEE YOU or YOU LOOK REALLY CUTE TODAY will sound kind because of how you say them, and that translates to I'M YOUR FRIEND in doggy language.

HOW TO APPROACH A DOG

There are some GOLDEN RULES to follow whenever you meet any new dog, or even dogs that you have known a long time:

ASK A GROWN-UP

Make sure there is a grown-up around whenever you are near a dog and ask before you approach one. They will know whether their dog wants to be stroked or not.

If the answer is no, you MUST NOT step any closer.

If the answer is yes, then stay calm and let the dog approach you. This is important, as we should always allow dogs to make their own choices too.

19

SAYING HELLO

If they want to come forward and say hello, say hello back by giving them a gentle stroke in one of the stroke zones.

It might help as well to follow my 'five, five, five' rule:

STEP ONE: Stroke five. Give a gentle stroke to say hello but make sure the stroke only lasts five seconds.

STEP TWO: Stop five. You must then stop stroking and keep your hands by your sides for five seconds. If the dog gives you a nudge with their nose, paws at you, chooses to stay by your side or is wiggling their bottom, these are all 'happy signs' that they give you permission to carry on.

20

However, if at any time they choose to walk away from you, don't follow them and instead let them be.

HIPS - JUST THE SPOT!

BACK - YES, PLEASE!

EARS - HMM, NOT REALLY.

TAIL - HANDS OFF!

CHIN - OOOH, YEAH!

FEET - NO WAY!

CHEST - A BIG YES!

BELLY - HMM, NO THANKS.

STEP THREE: Repeat five. You can repeat the 'stroke and stop' up to five times MAXIMUM before you must stop altogether and then move away. All dogs need a break after a while!

WHAT TO DO IF A DOG APPROACHES YOU FROM NOWHERE

If you are out and about and an unknown dog comes running over to you, you might feel a bit unsure. It probably just wants to say hello. But for those moments, I have three tips:

1 Don't scream and don't run.
I know it can feel scary – but the problem with screaming or running away is that the dog may see it as an invitation to play and start chasing!

2 Become a statue! Stand still, legs together, arms crossed over your chest, and take deep breaths in and out, staying quiet.
This immediately makes you a very 'boring'

human to a dog, which in this case is PERFECT. They may sniff you, they might even bark, but as long as you stay still and don't move, it is likely they will lose interest very quickly and go back to their owners.

3 If the owner is a long way away, stay calm and stay close to a grown-up. Tell them you feel worried, in a normal voice, without screaming ,and remember the 'statue rule'. The grown-up can hold the dog until the owner arrives.

TAIL TALK

We can learn a lot about a dog's mood by looking at the tail. I like to call it 'TAIL TALK' - and it gives us a quick clue as to what's going through a dog's mind.

TAIL HELD HIGH

When a dog's tail is held up high, wagging quickly from side to side, that is generally a sign that they are happy and excited!

I'M SO EXCITED!

WHAT DO YOU DO?

If the owner says it's OK, this dog likely wants you to 'TALK' back to them by saying hello. You might even give them a gentle stroke!

NEUTRAL TAIL

When a dog's tail is held at its 'starting point' or 'neutral', they are usually calm, relaxed and neither excited nor scared.

WHAT DO YOU DO?

This is a bit like when you are watching your FAVOURITE TELEVISION SHOW and you don't like to be interrupted. In other words, DO NOT DISTURB!

LOW TAIL

If a dog's tail is tucked tightly between their back legs, underneath them, and it isn't moving, they are most likely anxious, nervous or scared.

WHAT DO YOU DO?

The best thing to do is ask a grown-up to help. If the dog knows you, try talking

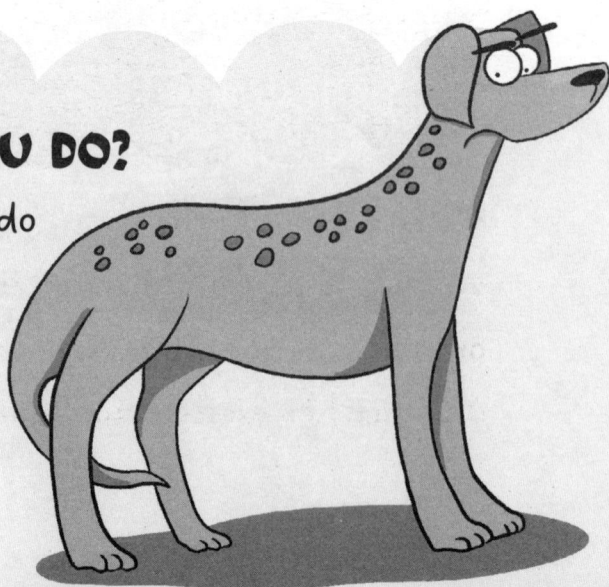

to them in a quiet, calm voice to help reassure them – but do not try to stroke, hug, comfort or move ANY dog that has a low tail.

STIFF TAIL

An unhappy dog will have its tail held straight, stiff and slightly raised. The tail will be shaking or wagging quickly, but this time, not because they are happy. A dog can bite even when they are wagging their tail.

WHAT DO YOU DO?

This dog is 'ON GUARD' and could lunge or bite a person if they come close. Do not try and talk to this dog or reassure them – instead keep your distance and stay with a grown-up.

THE HELICOPTER TAIL

A dog whose tail is swishing round and round in big, wide circles, like the propellers of a helicopter, while their bum is wiggling from side to side, is one marvellously happy hound. They are doing the happy dog dance!

WHAT DO YOU DO?

I think you just found a NEW BEST FRIEND! Don't forget we only want to talk to dogs in kind, calm, quiet voices, though – no screams or clapping hands to celebrate in case they suddenly get scared!

WE HAVE LIFT-OFF!

THE PLAY BOW

When a dog crouches to the ground on all fours with its bottom high up in the air, it is READY TO PLAY! It will usually be followed by zoomies!

WHAT DO YOU DO?

This will be a high-energy, zoomy dog. You might prefer to watch from a distance if they are particularly large (and bonkers!), or if the owner says it's OK, you might throw their ball for them to chase! THEY MIGHT EVEN GIVE YOU A DOGGY TREAT TO OFFER THEM! YUM!

THROW THE BALL!

THROW THE BALL!

Spinning round and round on the spot whilst trying to **bite their tails** could be a sign of some unwanted fleas making their fur itch, or more commonly it is probably something they just find quite fun! **In other words, it's a doggy boredom buster!**

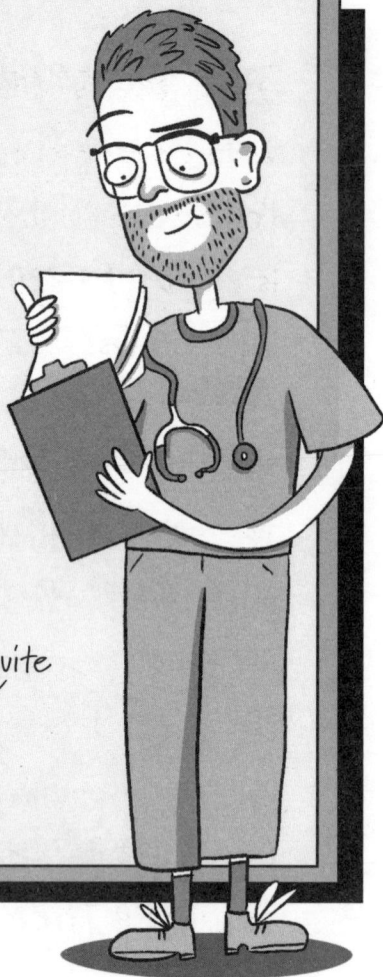

FACING FACTS

It's not just the tail that can help you communicate with your dog – you can look for clues in their faces too. Dogs can make a

whopping 100 different facial expressions to express how they feel! Here are some subtle signs you might recognise on a person which mean something very different on a dog:

YAWNING

Like us, dogs will yawn when they are tired. However, dogs will also yawn when they feel stressed or worried.

If they are yawning because they are nervous, I try talking to them. I ask them:

WHAT'S THE MATTER?

A calm voice can be VERY REASSURING to dogs.

Some dogs even yawn in an attempt to help calm themselves and the people around them! It's their way of trying to create a 'CHILL-OUT VIBE' when they think everyone's a bit nervous.

So try to show them 'calm signs' in return to help them RELAX – keep your hands by your side, don't try to hug or kiss them, and don't try to talk to them face-to-face, as they may mistake this for a scary stare.

LIP LICKING

Nom nom nom, tasty snack incoming! It is true that dogs will lick their lips (or drool) when food is on its way, but they can also lick their lips or quickly stick their tongues out when they feel scared or they feel sick.

They aren't saying:

> I WANT TO LICK YOU.

They are saying:

> I FEEL A BIT NERVOUS.

or

> I'VE GOT BELLY ACHE AND MIGHT THROW UP!

The best way to help them in this case is to calmly reassure them using a quiet voice and tell a grown-up you think they might be feeling a bit sick or nervous. These dogs often need a bit of space, so try to not 'crowd round' them and instead watch from a distance.

ASK JAMES:
Can you talk to a dog through food?

Playing lots of **treasure hunt games**, using **puzzle feeders** and **scattering some treats in a rolled-up towel** is a fun way to talk to your dog as they LOVE **solving puzzles** and getting a treat as a reward! It's also a great way to train them. When they're first learning to use the toilet outside or you want them to come back to you on a walk, giving a treat as a reward can show them that good behaviour results in tasty things!

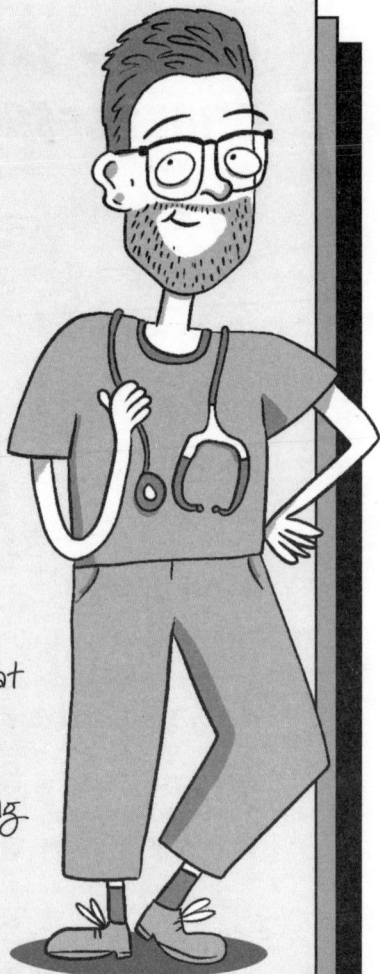

SMILE - SAY CHEEEEEESE!

HOLD YOUR HORSES - a smile isn't always what it seems!

'THIS IS NOT THE TIME FOR PHOTOS, THANKS!'

Sometimes dogs pull their lips back and show their teeth, not because they're getting ready to take a quick selfie but as a warning sign that they are unhappy.

This dog is giving a *WARNING SIGNAL* that they *MIGHT* bite. Step away, respect their warning sign and find a grown-up.

34

SIDE EYE

Some dogs can serve up some SERIOUS SIDE EYE! It is their way of saying:

PLEASE BACK OFF!

This is also called 'whale eye' because they keep their eyes fixed on something without moving their heads, revealing the white part of their eye – making them look a bit like a whale. In this situation, we must move away and give them space.

ASK JAMES:
If a dog lies on their back to show you their belly, does that mean they want some belly rubs?

Hmmmm, sometimes yes, but **more commonly no**. If they are showing other relaxed signs, it can mean they are **happy to be stroked** and it is the ultimate **sign of trust**. But if this is a dog you have not met before or they are in unfamiliar surroundings, it might be a way of them saying, **'I feel worried and I'm showing you my belly to indicate that I am not a threat, but I also don't want any attention,'** and we need to respect that.

BARK TIME

What can a dog's bark tell us? **DIFFERENT BARK SOUNDS CAN MEAN DIFFERENT THINGS.** Here are some examples:

ARRRRRRR-ROOFF

can mean

I WANNA PLAY!

Whether it's chasing a ball or heading out for a walk, this is a happy dog that wants some attention.

RAFF-RAFF

can mean

I'M HUNGRY!

This is often in **ANTICIPATION OF FOOD**; however, be warned, if you give in to a dog's demands, they will quickly learn that barking lots gets them treats! You might be better to instead try playing a game with them or distract them with some training.

A deep

OOOOF-OOOOOOOF-OOOOOOOOF!

is often a **WARNING SIGNAL** that the dog is not happy. Respond to this by stepping away and stay close to a grown-up.

AROOOOOOOOOOOOO

is your typical 'WOLF HOWL'. This dog might be bored and need more exercise, or they might struggle with being left on their own. Respond by seeking help from a professional dog behaviourist to help build up their independence.

So now that you know what your dog is trying to say, WHY NOT TALK BACK TO THEM TOO? But remember, you can't judge a dog's mood by just one feature.

If we want to talk back, we have to look at their WHOLE body to work out how they are feeling. Why not take a look at the ladder of communication?

BITE

SNAP

GROWL

STIFFENING UP OR STARING

LYING DOWN, STAYING VERY
STILL, SHOWING THEIR BELLY

CROUCHING DOWN WITH TAIL
TUCKED UNDERNEATH THEM

EARS BACK, LICKING LIPS,
CREEPING AWAY

WALKING AWAY

WHOLE BODY TURNING AWAY

LOOKING AWAY

YAWNING, BLINKING,
LICKING THEIR OWN NOSE

I use this all the time to help me understand a dog's mood. The signs at the bottom of the ladder show a dog who is feeling a little bit worried, and as we move up the ladder, they are showing clues that they feel increasingly scared, anxious and unhappy.

All of the clues – from bottom to top – show the dog is asking for some space. The earlier we back off, the less likely they are to reach 'growl', 'snap' or 'bite'.

Remember, though, reading a dog's mood can be really tricky, so always make sure you have a grown-up to help at all times.

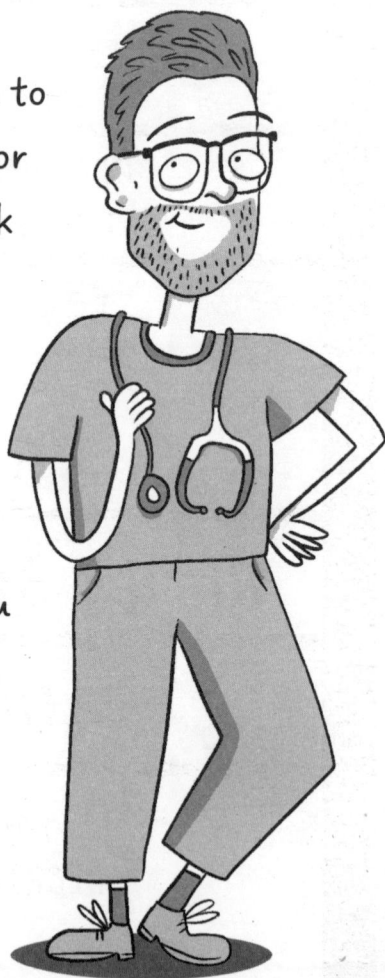

DOLLY'S DOS AND DON'TS

✓ DO always ask an owner before petting a dog and follow the answer they give.

✗ DON'T automatically assume every dog wants to be stroked, even dogs you know.

✓ DO stay calm if a dog approaches you on a walk – think, 'STATUE!'

✗ DON'T always assume a wagging tail means the dog is in a happy mood.

✓ DO learn how to read a dog's body language.

✗ DON'T ever punish a dog – it will only scare them!

CHAPTER TWO

CATS

I'm going to let you in on a HUGE secret. Cats can read your mind AND predict your every move! YOU HEARD IT HERE FIRST, EVERYONE! The cat is FINALLY out of the bag! Well, OK, perhaps they can't predict EVERY move, but cats do pick up on lots of different cues from us.

Have you ever heard someone say, 'I DON'T REALLY LIKE CATS BUT THEY ALWAYS COME TO ME!'? Well, this is true. Cats will often walk straight to the people who like them least. It's all to do with human behaviour. The human who doesn't like cats often STAYS STILL when a cat enters

the room. Whereas most other humans who do like cats immediately start to make **FUNNY NOISES** or **RUB THEIR THUMBS AND FINGERS TOGETHER** to try and get the cat's attention.

NONE OF THESE THINGS MEAN ANYTHING IN CAT LANGUAGE, and from their point of view, the human that stays still is the one that is **PURRFECTLY BEHAVED!**

Another thing that says, '**I'M A FRIENDLY HUMAN,**' in cat language is **OUR OWN FACIAL EXPRESSION.** The most important thing is NOT TO STARE! Instead, try half closing your eyes and every so often blinking and turning your head away from them. This is called a '**SLOW BLINK**'. It is a way of saying, 'I am not a threat.' You might even find your cat does the same back!

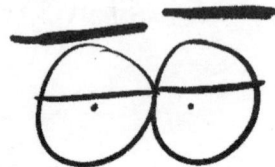

CAT MOODS

There are loads of body language signs that will tell you if a cat is happy, anxious or feeling threatened and angry – they're a great way to communicate with your cat.

HAPPY CATS WILL:

- Calmly walk towards you, with their heads lifted

- Have their eyes half closed in a rugby ball shape

- Have their tail high up in the air with a small curve at the tip

- Roll on to their back by your feet (but this is NOT an invitation for belly rubs!)

Blink slowly at you

Hop up on to your lap

Groom themselves in front of you

If you see a cat doing any of these things, they're showing a lot of relaxed signs and are likely comfortable in your presence.

ANXIOUS CATS WILL:

🐾 Stay still

🐾 Crouch low to the ground

🐾 Keep close watch on everything happening around them

🐾 Have their eyes fully open in a football shape

🐾 Choose to hide away rather than greet you

STAY AWAY, PLEASE!

🐾 Have their ears low and flat against their head

If you see a cat doing any of these, they are feeling a little unsure. They need some more time to observe and investigate before they decide whether they trust you yet. Don't see this as a fail, though – see it as your golden opportunity to prove you can 'speak cat' by letting your body do the talking and keeping very quiet. Crouch down, don't stare, make no sudden movements and just let them come to you.

IF I STAY REALLY STILL...

I MIGHT GO AND SAY HELLO.

ANGRY CATS WILL:

Hsssssss!

🐾 Stay still

🐾 Make themselves look big and fierce, often arching their backs

🐾 Puff their fur out

🐾 Have their eyes big and wide

- Make their whiskers face forward
- Keep their tail high and tense, not swaying
- Make a hissing sound
- Take a swipe with their claws or maybe bite

NOT HAPPY!

If a cat does this, they are feeling angry, scared or even threatened. DO NOT TRY TO APPROACH – instead, stay back, stay still, stay quiet and get help from a grown-up.

ASK JAMES:
Is purring like talking?

Most cats purr when they are **feeling cosy** and **comfortable**. But they can also purr when they feel nervous, if they are in pain or to try and calm themselves down. There are even some studies showing that cats with **injuries can heal faster if they purr**, which might be due to the **healing vibrations** travelling through their bodies! **PRETTY NEAT!** So, in a way, they are talking, as they're giving us lots of information!

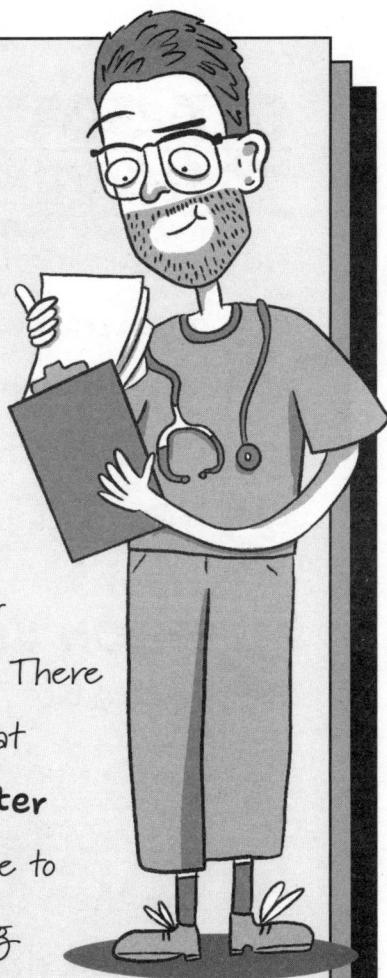

CAT GOT YOUR TONGUE?

Kittens meow all the time to their siblings and mothers, but adult cats don't meow to each other much at all. However, cats DO meow towards their humans quite often.
BUT WHAT DOES IT ALL MEAN?

MEOW ON REPEAT

This can mean a cat is excited and looking forward to something - usually some food! Think twice before giving in to their protests! Offering them some food could accidentally 'reward' their demands for snacks!

MEOWWW

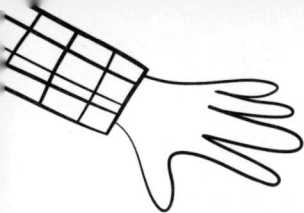

My advice would be to offer up some extra chin tickles or reach for a toy and start a game with them.

A GROWLY MEOW

A GROWLY MEOW means the cat is NOT HAPPY – they might be protecting their food or feel threatened by another cat or just not want any attention right now. They are giving a WARNING SIGNAL that they are not happy about something. Stay back, stay quiet and stay still.

THE SHORT MEOW

These are short 'MEW' sounds that often happen first thing in the morning or if your cat hasn't seen you for

MEW MEW

54

a while. If your cat says, 'Good morning,' you need to say it back! I find a few minutes of 'cat chat' puts everyone in a good mood to start the day!

THE YOWL

Meooooooooooow

A long, low-pitched 'YOWLING' meow can indicate a medical issue, discomfort or worry. A change in your cat's meow might not seem like such a big deal but can be a really USEFUL CLUE that they might be feeling poorly or not quite themselves. If you notice a change in their meow, it is important to tell a grown-up who can arrange a trip to the vet.

HEADS OR TAILS
(OR PAWS OR WHISKERS!)?

Did you know that cats can also tell you what they want with their tail, head and paws?

TAIL

🐾 Flicking quickly from side to side: The cat is in problem-solving mode and trying to investigate something – leave them to it until they have completed their mission!

🐾 Hairs standing up like a toilet brush: This is a cat that could be about to attack! DO NOT APPROACH, as they may scratch or bite!

🐾 Tucked underneath them: A cat might tuck their tail when they are curled up, snoozing, and that's normal. But if they are walking or running with their tail tucked underneath them it's because they are scared – they need space.

Straight up with a curl at the tip: The cat is feeling pretty content and relaxed, and they are exploring or ready to play.

HEAD

Headbutting: They are stamping their scent on you to claim you as their own, and it is a mark of affection and trust. Offer a chin tickle or head stroke, which is a simple way to say, 'I trust you,' back.

Rubbing: A cat that rubs its head or body around your ankles or feet is saying hello. This is normal behaviour for most cats and tends to be a 'happy' sign.

Face sniffing: This is their way of getting as much information about us as possible, even down to the smell of our breath. If a cat is trying to sniff your face, I'd suggest gently offering your jumper or hand to sniff instead, so they can still get all the information they need!

Licking: When cats lick us, it is not because they like the taste. It is a bonding exercise. They want us to smell of their saliva. It feels good to them and makes them feel happy and relaxed. Don't worry, you don't have to lick them back!

IMPORTANT NOTE: Some cats may feel so relaxed that they wake with a start, jump off your lap and run away. This is called the 'startle reaction' and it is when cats panic that they have relaxed too much and suddenly feel a bit vulnerable. They may also start to lick their paws straight after, which is a bit like them saying:

I'M SORRY – I DIDN'T REALLY MEAN TO DO IT.

Cats can also suddenly bite at the same time as them licking you. This can come from nowhere and be a BIT OF A SURPRISE! It's usually a sign your cat is OVERSTIMULATED or OVER-EXCITED! Try to increase playtime with hunting-type toys, don't stroke them for too long at any one time – stick to one- or two-minute bursts – and only stroke them in their stroke zones.

HEAD –
I'LL LET YOU BUT
IT'S NOT MY FAVE.

RUMP –
OOOH, THIS IS
PURRRFECT!

CHIN –
A BIG YES –
THIS IS THE WINNER.

TAIL –
WOAH,
NO WAY!

FEET –
NOPE!

BELLY –
YOU MIGHT REGRET IT!

PAWS

🐾 Kneading: If a cat kneads you (like a baker making bread!), it is a sign they think of you as their mother. It is the ultimate sign of love and affection!

🐾 Clawing: Scratchy claws, on the other hand, could be a signal to 'back off'. It can also be a signal to say, 'I've had enough of being stroked.' It might also indicate your cat is in pain and may need a trip to the vet. Always tell a grown-up if you get scratched.

🐾 Batting: If a cat bats you with their paw, it is them literally tapping you to say:

OI, PAY ME SOME ATTENTION!

WHISKERS

Cats have around TWENTY-FOUR WHISKERS in total on their muzzle, above their eyes and on their cheeks. They also have some on the BACKS OF THEIR FRONT LEGS! Cats use their whiskers to work out what's happening directly in front of them, how wide a gap is (to tell if the rest of their bodies will fit through) and even which way the wind is blowing! For all these reasons, it's super important to NEVER trim a cat's whiskers. One final role of the whiskers is in COMMUNICATION.

🐾 Whiskers drooping to the side: This is the neutral position, which shows that a cat is relaxed and calm.

Whiskers pointing forward:
They are in 'investigation
mode'! The cat is
curious, excited
or researching
something new.
If they hold
their whiskers in this
position for a long time, it
could also indicate that they
are in pain — so you may need
to ask a grown-up to call the vet.

Whiskers pulled back against the face: This
means they feel scared or worried about
something. Allow them to hide away and
calm down, and try to work out and
remove whatever it was they
were feeling scared of.

TALKING BACK

You can *TALK BACK* to your cat by keeping them entertained and making them feel comfortable round the house.

Here are some ideas:

🐾 Get creative with puzzle feeders and interactive food toys, and play lots of hunting games.

🐾 Separate feeding stations, water stations and litter trays as much as possible. Cats don't like their water bowl being next to their food bowl, and they certainly don't want to go to the toilet right next to where they eat!

🐾 Dedicate an area for them to hide in and place a 'do not disturb' sign outside!

PLEASE DO NOT DISTURB

🐾 Cats often like to be able to 'smell' us as they sleep, as a way to help them feel secure. A cardboard box can work perfectly well as a bed, so fold an old jumper you no longer wear into the box to add a touch of scented luxury to their bedding! It'll be like you're 'talking' to them all night long.

🐾 Scratching posts are essential for all cats to exercise, stretch, sharpen their claws and transfer scent.

SCRATCH

SCRITCH

SCRITCH

SCRATCH

SCRATCH

THE PET FILES

All cats enjoy showing off their hunting prowess,
no matter how good they are at it. It is a good
idea to play games with them that tap into these feline
super-skills. Try using fishing rod toys whilst flicking some
treats to simulate chasing prey. Or, at meal times, use
puzzle feeders so your cat has to work out how
to get their dinner. Don't forget, cats love to climb so try
placing some treats off the ground, perhaps along the
backof a sofa – they have AMAZING balance!

Water is very good for cats. It helps keep their
kidneys and wee healthy. So, ideally, it would be great
if our fabulous felines would take a few extra sips of the
good stuff. Cats don't like getting their whiskers wet!
So try offering water in a flat saucer, from a dripping
tap or an electric water fountain, or even leave some
bowls outside to see if they prefer the flavour of
rain more than tap water!

ASK JAMES:
Can cats drink milk?

Whilst cats love the taste and texture of milk and cream, they are **lactose intolerant**, which means anything containing cows' milk may cause vomiting or diarrhoea. Milk also contains a lot of phosphate, which can damage the kidneys. **All in all, it's best to avoid.**

MASTERS OF DISGUISE

Cats will rarely show it when they feel poorly or are in pain. They tend to just . . . stop . . . and stay still or sleep more.

But we can tell by a cat's facial expression if they are in pain – they sort of 'screw' their faces up, their eyes close a bit, their whiskers are held straight out rather than flopping downwards, their ears are flat instead of pointing upwards and their muzzle is tense and clenched.

If you ever feel that a cat seems 'quieter' than usual, or just 'not quite right' – then trust your gut instinct and ask a grown-up to call the vet.

DOLLY'S DOS AND DON'TS

[X] DON'T make the first move! Cats like to feel in control of their own choices, so let them decide to say hello first.

[✓] DO listen out for their sounds – a meow, hiss or a purr all mean different things.

[X] DON'T stare into their eyes – instead, mimic their slow blink and slowly turn your head away.

[✓] DO always talk quietly around cats.

[X] DON'T make any sudden movements.

TALLY-HO!

During the Victorian era, pet rabbits were put in tiny cages so people could stare at them up close. We've come a long way since then, but we do still think it's normal for a rabbit to live in a small hutch. To understand their feelings, we need to start by offering a much BIGGER HOUSE. We must also make sure bunnies aren't housed alone. They need other bunnies around them to thrive. A bunny on its own will feel like it always needs to be on high alert. Rabbits don't literally talk, but that doesn't mean they can't show how they're feeling.

70

HAPPY

If a rabbit RESTS and RELAXES in front of you by lying down and stretching out, or exploring and even eating, then you're off to a good start. Listen out for occasional sounds – happy rabbits 'PURR' like cats or make a CLUCKING SOUND. You may even hear them sigh – which is not a sign of boredom but a sign that they are feeling really content. Oh, also, the CUTEST sign to look out for in a happy bunny is them twitching their nose lots!

THUMP

THUMP

WORRIED

A worried bunny will stay still, appear small and hunched up, flatten their ears against their heads and try to hide (or run away from you). The nose doesn't twitch when bunnies are worried, and instead you might hear their back foot make a sudden 'thumping' sound against the ground. This is a warning sign to their other rabbit friends that there is danger nearby. If you are seeing these signs, it's best to allow your rabbit to hide away.

ANGRY

Rabbits that feel THREATENED or SCARED can resort to aggression as a last resort in self-defence. They will crouch but look tense, as though they're about to fight, and

sometimes will stand on their back legs with their fists out, ready to have a boxing match. They can sometimes make a growl, grunt or even screaming sound.

It is worth a trip to the vet to check there's nothing wrong, and it's a good idea to review their home life – maybe they're not getting on with the other rabbits, or maybe they need more space.

BINKY

You might have heard about dogs having the 'ZOOMIES' – but did you know that rabbits get the 'BINKIES'? A binky is a

sign of an EXTREMELY HAPPY and CONTENT rabbit. When they're running around (or sometimes just standing still) they suddenly leap up into the air and twist their head and bodies in opposite directions! It's their version of doing a heel-click jump in the middle of a musical stage play – THEY ARE QUITE LITERALLY JUMPING FOR JOY!

DO RABBITS WANT TO BE PICKED UP?

In the wild, rabbits are prey animals, so the only time they would naturally be lifted off the ground is if they are being attacked. Of course, we pose no threat to them, but

sometimes their NATURAL INSTINCTS may kick in and they SUDDENLY PANIC. Most bunnies would rather have playtime on the floor or close to the ground, so if you can, it might be best for you to sit on the floor and stroke or play with them next to you, especially if you have other friends round (of the human variety!).

If you do need to pick them up, the best way is to hold them close into your body and use both hands, one supporting under the chest and back end and the other over the shoulders. NEVER pick a rabbit up by grabbing the skin around its neck,

NEVER hold a rabbit by its ears and NEVER turn a rabbit on to its back. These are all painful, old-fashioned ways of holding rabbits and are considered cruel.

THE PET FILES

Did you know that rabbits eat their own poo? It might sound disgusting – well, it IS – but they do so for an important reason. Rabbits don't get all the nutrients they need from their food in one go. In order to extract everything they need from their plant-based diet, the food needs to pass through twice!

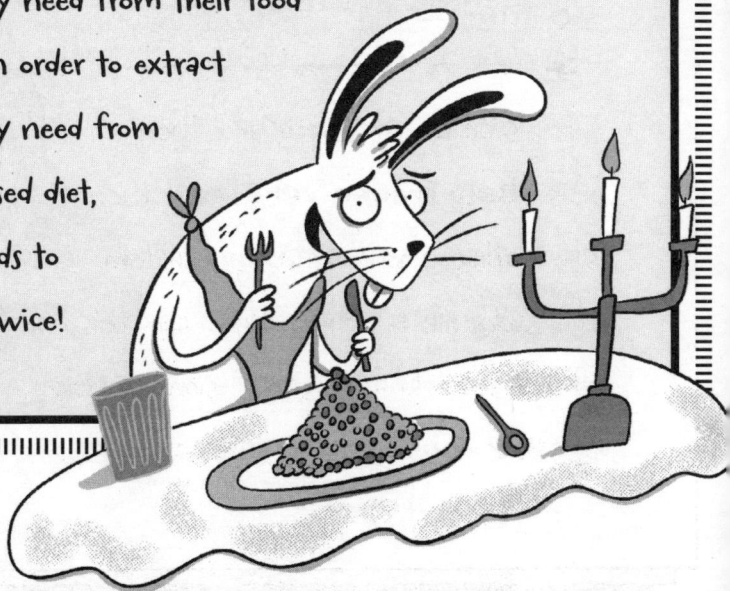

DIET

Bunnies are vegan, so it would make sense for us to feed them lots of fruit and veg, right? WRONG! Rabbits need lots and lots of scratchy fibre, like hay, to keep their guts healthy. In fact, a rabbit could exist entirely on a diet of hay, grass and water! Crazy, huh?

ASK JAMES:
What happens if a bunny skips a meal or stops eating altogether?

This is an **emergency** and they need **help from a vet**. When they stop eating, their entire gut system will suddenly fall out of sync and this can quickly lead to a dangerous slowing down of their **continuous poo-factory**.

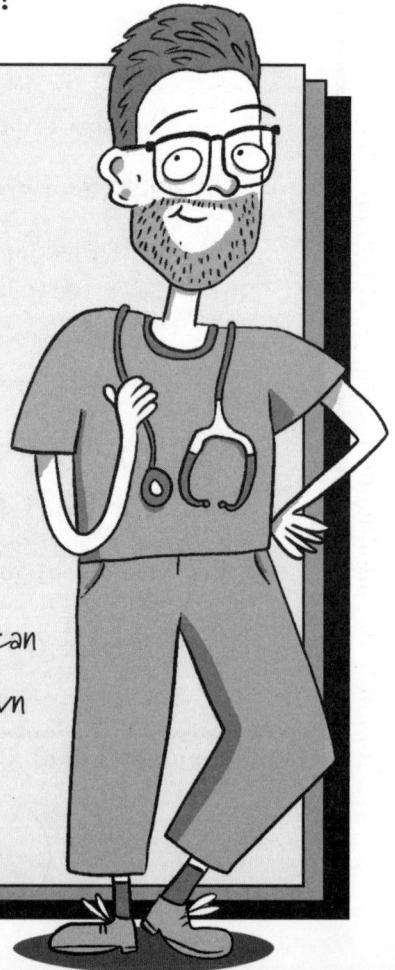

BUSY BUNNIES

Rabbits spend hours searching for food in the wild and we can replicate this for them as pets. Here are some ideas:

- Willow sticks or apple tree branches are suitable to give rabbits to gnaw on and play with. Just avoid anything that has high sugar content.

- Rabbits love running through tunnels — try cutting a hole at the front and back of a few large cardboard boxes and watch as your rabbits zoom in and out of them!

- Try filling a paper bag or empty cardboard egg carton with some hay, a few pieces of pelleted food and a few strands of some fresh herbs like parsley or dill, then fold over the open end and watch as your bunnies rip and dig their way through to find the tasty herby snacks!

A handful of freshly picked grass or some dandelion leaves, raspberry leaves or apple tree twigs are all healthy options. Always give them a good wash under the tap beforehand, double-check you have identified the correct plants and NEVER give them clippings from a lawn-mower! These start to rot very quickly and may have dangerous petrol or chemicals on them.

HOW TO CHECK YOUR BUNNY OVER

Bunnies can become really poorly very quickly, so we have to keep a close eye out to make sure they're OK. Here are some signs to look for:

EYES: Should be clean and bright with no discharge. If you see a white, sticky, glue-like substance in a bunny's eyes or the fur starts clumping on the side of their face, then that is not normal.

EARS: Should be clear of any debris. Lots of earwax, head shaking or tilting their head to one side are signs of concern.

NOSE: When bunnies breathe, it is almost completely silent! You should not hear any rattly noises or sneezing, or see any crusty snot around their nose.

TEETH: Rabbits have twenty-eight teeth! Regular vet dental check-ups are essential. The teeth should all be aligned and not pointing in an inward or outward direction. If you see drooling, feel hard lumps along the jawbone or notice them going off their food, these could all be signs of dental pain.

CHOMP

BOTTOMS: It is important to check rabbits' bottoms every day to make sure there is no poo stuck to the fur. Any big poo clumps could indicate gut problems, a tooth problem or even painful joints. Clumps of poo can also attract flies and lead to a life-threatening condition called flystrike!

PRRRRP!

THE PET FILES

Did you know that rabbits' teeth never stop growing? This means they can chew and chew to their heart's content and their teeth will never wear away! HOWEVER, it also means if rabbits don't eat enough hay, their teeth can overgrow into huge, painful sharp spikes that cause all sorts of problems.

So make sure they eat LOTS of it!

DOLLY'S DOS AND DON'TS

[X] DON'T mix rabbits with other species such as guinea pigs.

[✓] DO consider how to best house your rabbits – they need lots of space and friends!

[X] DON'T feed them too many treats – remember HAY, HAY, HAY!

[✓] DO make sure you check your bunnies over every single day.

[X] DON'T ignore if a bunny skips a meal or doesn't do a poo – call the vet immediately.

DOLLY

I've got a really cool fact about chickens.
READY? CHICKENS ARE, IN FACT, MODERN-
DAY, LIVING DINOSAURS.

WHY DID THE DINOSAUR
CROSS THE ROAD?

BECAUSE CHICKENS
WEREN'T AROUND YET!

Of course, chickens weren't around when
the actual dinosaurs roamed the planet,
but birds are considered to be the DIRECT
DESCENDANTS OF OUR DINOSAUR FRIENDS.

The velociraptor had **FEATHERS**, and clever science people have discovered that there are some other **VERY SIMILAR CHARACTERISTICS BETWEEN CHICKENS AND DINOSAURS** – which is why many people agree that chickens are, in fact, just smaller, less fierce dinosaur pets. WOW!

There aren't many pets in this book (**OR THE ENTIRE UNIVERSE, FOR THAT MATTER**) that produce things from their bottoms you can **EAT** (eww!) – but chickens and their egg-laying super-skills are the one **BRILLIANT EXCEPTION.** Our feathered friends are one of my favourite animals on the planet!

CHICKEN, HEN, COCKEREL, CHOOK, ROOSTER - WHAT'S WHAT AND WHO'S WHO?

If you want to know how to talk to a chicken, it's important to get its name right first! Just so you know, a hen is a female chicken, whilst a cockerel (or rooster) is a male chicken. A chicken or chook is a general term for either. When people say they have 'chickens', what they often mean is they have hens.

Cockerels cannot be kept with other cockerels – they can be quite aggressive and will fight (really fight – they have big claws on their ankles which are sharp and can cause some serious pet-ninja damage). They are also known to be **VERY** loud and **VERY** early risers!

Once cockerels start talking, everyone can hear!

COCK-A-DOODLE-DOOOO!

CHICKEN BASICS

Chickens DO make wonderful pets, but they also have some very specific wants and needs. They aren't the right pet for everyone.

Chickens need outdoor space, and they also need a henhouse to live in. Most people start with a 'CHICKEN COOP' – this tends to have a raised house section with an attached exercise run that can be picked up and moved

around on to fresh ground. It should be well made and easy to clean, with nesting boxes for the chickens to lay their eggs in, a perch for them to sleep on and a lockable door to keep them safe at night from predators. Exactly how much space they need will depend on how many hens there are (HENS CANNOT BE KEPT ON THEIR OWN!) but as a general rule – THE MORE SPACE THE BETTER.

They will need an area to scratch about in, a dust bath to powder their feathers in, pelleted chicken food, fresh daily water and a bowl of special grit for them to peck, which helps them to digest their food and make shells for their eggs. Chickens don't like the rain – and they can't use umbrellas – so they'll also need somewhere to shelter in stormy weather.

Chickens are **EXTREMELY CLEVER** – they will know to return to their house at dusk and put themselves to bed. 'Roosting' is how chickens sleep – they like to find a nice high perch, then line up side by side and sleep together in a row. They don't like to sleep on the ground because, firstly, there is a higher chance of predators and, secondly – poo! Chickens will usually poo whenever and wherever they need!

If they're on a perch, the poo will literally 'drop' to the floor beneath them – which is why chicken poo is sometimes called 'droppings' - so they don't have to worry about waking up in a flustered feathery mess!

THE PET FILES

Chickens don't have a bladder, which means their poo and pee all come out mixed together in one super-dump of chicken plop.

HOW TO HANDLE A CHICKEN

Some chickens don't mind being picked up, but some really don't like it. However, it's worth getting them used to being handled, to check them over for any signs of illness. To do so, slide an arm underneath them, clamp your fingers gently around their legs and support their weight on the length of your forearm. You want them to rest with their face pointing towards your armpit.

NEVER grab a hen or lift them by their legs, as it can dislocate their hip joints. OUCH!

HOW TO MAKE FRIENDS WITH A CHICKEN

It's very easy to tame pet chickens as they LOVE food! Once they get to know you and realise you bring them food, they'll be so excited to see you!

Most chickens are too heavy to fly, so when they hear you arrive, they run as fast as they can, hopping from foot to foot at full speed towards you – channelling their inner dino skills, like a T. rex running at full pelt!

Here are some tips for talking to your chicken friends whilst feeding them:

✔ Start slow and crouch low! If your hens start off a little shy, grab a handful of their food and gently toss it in their direction. Eventually they will link you with food and realise you are a friend, not a threat.

✔ Train them by saying a single phrase at the same time as feeding them. Maybe:

BWAAAAWK!

Or something a bit more posh and refined, like:

COME ALONG NOW!

Very soon they will think of you as their hen-butler who brings them food and will come running as soon as they hear you!

✔ Don't be surprised if they recognise you! Hens can recognise 100 different faces, so they will definitely know it is you when you arrive! They will soon happily peck food straight from your hand, sit down beside you or rub their beak against you! You'll be firm friends in no time.

✔ Use each hen's individual name — you will be surprised how quickly they can tell when you are talking to them each in turn.

✔ Chat away to them — hens love a good gossip. Ask them how their day was, find out what's been happening and you will soon be surrounded by chicken chitter-chatter as your hens chat back.

MY DAY WAS EGGSELLENT!

✔ Practise your karaoke - warm up the vocal cords and belt out a few tunes for them. Hens love to hear a good sing-song.

ASK JAMES:
Can I play games with chickens?

If you're looking for a fun game to play with your chickens, they love **HIDE-AND-SEEK**. Try hiding around a corner with some treats and calling out their names one by one to see if they can find you. **Their prize is a tasty treat!**

ASK JAMES:
Do you need to wash a hen's eggs?

No! You definitely shouldn't.

They have a special protein coating which helps to prevent bacteria getting through the shell. Washing or scrubbing eggs in water damages this layer and can lead to them going off.

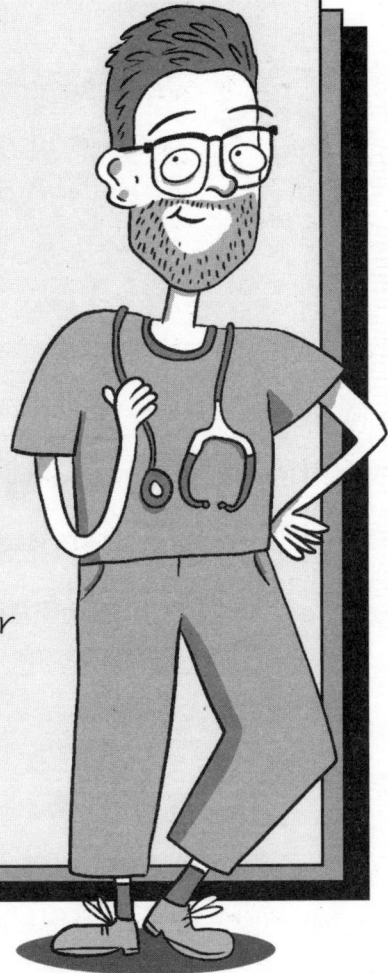

THE PET FILES

Even though it may sound painful to us, laying an egg is not thought to be painful for chickens. It takes twenty-five hours in total for an egg to grow from start to finish. In fact, chickens even sing an 'egg song' to celebrate — telling all their friends they've just laid another top-notch egg! What an achievement!

TIME FOR A HEN PARTY!

Happy hens are those that get to experience everything their jungle-dwelling ancestors did — so here are a few ideas:

✔ If you have a garden, try letting your chickens run free for a short while — they'll love scratching through the soil to find tasty worms and bugs!

✓ Collect up some fallen leaves and sprinkle some hen food over them. Your hens will LOVE rummaging through, pecking on some snacks.

✓ Try hanging up anything that reflects light — small mirrors, old DVDs, maybe even a disco ball. The shimmering lights look like insect wings to chickens — so they will chase after the reflections and peck at the treats!

✓ Hens LOVE music and tinkly sounds from wind chimes. Try playing some soothing classical music and you may even see them lay a few more eggs to say thank you!

✓ Finally, don't forget to train your dinosaurs! You can't toilet train your dino-pets, BUT you can train chickens to know their own names, complete puzzles and obstacle courses and do tricks.

IMPORTANT NOTE: You must NEVER feed pet chickens any leftover scraps or vegetable peelings from your kitchen. There is a risk of contamination and spreading disease.

Finally, hens can sometimes become quite unfriendly towards each other. There is a little bit of T. rex left in even the most docile of chickens!

Bullying is often a sign of boredom – so how can we help prevent bullying? By giving them EVEN MORE of what they want! Create their mini jungle play area with even more space, more toys and more hiding places, and don't forget the disco ball!

DOLLY'S DOS AND DON'TS

✓ DO provide your chickens with lots of activities.

✗ DON'T keep chickens on their own. They need friends – 3 together is the minimum!

✓ DO provide a nesting area for them to lay their delicious eggs.

✗ DON'T forget the henhouse-keeping – they poo A LOT!

✓ DO talk to your chickens – they love a gossip!

✗ DON'T forget to tell your friends you have a pet dinosaur!

CHAPTER FIVE

GUINEA PIGS

I can't start talking about guinea pigs without first addressing the big issue: **THEIR NAME!**

Why on earth are guinea pigs called guinea pigs? They don't come from Guinea and they are not related to pigs!

Some say they cost 'one guinea' – an old type of money – when they first arrived in England in the sixteenth century, but why pig? Honestly, whoever was in charge of naming pets in the olden days must have got all their paperwork mixed up or something, because my mind is totally boggled. But however they got their name, we do know what they want and how to talk to them!

BREEDS

Guinea pigs are super-popular pets, and depending on which country you live in, there are lots of different breeds. There are:

AMERICAN GUINEA PIGS: The original guinea piggy! It's been around the longest, is the most popular breed, is friendly and has a short, smooth coat that can have lots of different colours and markings.

MEEP

MEEP

MEEP

ABYSSINIAN GUINEA PIGS: These piggies have the ultimate 'bed-head' hairdo! Their coat grows in swirls called 'rosettes'. They can 'feel' it more when we stroke them and can be very sensitive to touch, which makes them shy, initially.

MEEP

PERUVIAN GUINEA PIGS:

These are a popular long-haired breed of piggy, with long locks flowing as though they have come straight from a shampoo advert! They are super friendly but they need daily grooming.

MEEP

MEEP *MEEP*

TEXEL GUINEA PIGS:

These guys have an impressive coat of curly, wavy hair, which needs lots of grooming. They are very friendly but not for beginners.

SKINNY PIGS:

These little piggies have no hair at all! However, despite looking like pocket-sized hippos, they are very sensitive. They can get sunburnt easily in the summer and can get very cold in the winter. They need lots of looking after.

MEEP

MEEP

Pet guinea pigs, as we know them, aren't really found in the wild as such – but there are some wild relatives that we can learn from. These wild 'guinea pigs' live in social groups and live off an entirely plant-based diet. Being a prey species, they have developed two survival instincts when faced with danger:

FREEZE! And pretend to be dead.

OR

SCATTER (where every guinea pig runs in different directions to confuse and escape the predator).

This is perhaps why even tame pet guinea pigs might run away if they think we are trying to catch them! Guinea pigs are crepuscular – that means they are most active at dawn and dusk – and they originate from the Andes mountains of South America.

THE PET FILES

Guinea pigs were first kept as pets in 5000 BCE by the people called the Incas, but it took Queen Elizabeth I to really put them on the map in England. Fascinated by their different coat types and colours, she kept guinea pigs as pets, giving them a royal seal of approval, which is possibly what launched them as one of the most popular pets even today!

CHATTER BOXES

Wild guinea pig live in social groups – and our domesticated guinea pigs want to do exactly the same. Guinea pigs like having other guinea pig housemates to share their lives with – they need to be kept in at least a pair, and they really don't want to live with rabbits.

BUT WHAT ON EARTH ARE GUINEA PIGS SAYING? And how are they trying to talk to us?

CHUTTERING

This is a nibbly, chirrupy kind of sound! Guinea pigs love a good natter, so talk back in jolly tones and tell them all about your day.

WHEEKING

When guinea pigs make a

WHEEEEEEEK, WHEEEEEEEEK, WHEEEEEEEK

sound, this is
them shouting:

FEED ME NOW!

Rather than just offering the food, try
linking it with some training! Use a gentle
command like, 'Here piggies!' then give them
the food as a reward. Soon you'll be able to
lead them anywhere you want them to go!

WHINING

A guinea pig's whine is a high-pitched groaning sound. It means they're unhappy or potentially unwell. So if it keeps happening, you might want to arrange a trip to the vet. However, they can also use that sound when they have finished their dinner and want a second helping, but unless it's hay or water, don't fall for their piggy protests!

TEETH GRINDING

Piggies grind their teeth when they are feeling a little unsure or anxious. You can sometimes hear them making a grating sound too. Sometimes a small, healthy treat will help make them feel better, or they might need to run into their hidey place until they feel a little more confident. Provide them with hiding places and don't follow them – they need a little time out to feel safe again.

POPCORNING

When guinea pigs are happy, they JUMP FOR JOY! It's called POPCORNING, and it is a sign that a guinea pig is feeling full of happiness and excitement.

When you spot your guinea pig jumping up in the air, you'll know you are DEFINITELY giving your pet EXACTLY what they want!

It can be really rewarding to know you've made them so happy, but try not to make any noise or clap as it could scare them! Instead, give yourself a quiet pat on the back!

DIET

Like lots of the furry friends we meet in this book, our piggy pals also require plenty of fresh hay.

It should make up around 90% of their daily diet, and as a rough guide each pig will eat around its own body size worth of hay EVERY DAY!

NOM NOM

They also need small amounts of pelleted food, some fresh veggies as treats and lots of vitamin C.

HOT HOT HOT

If temperatures soar above 20–25 degrees, then you need to keep your guinea pigs cool.

Keep them in their enclosure in the shade, or even move them into a cool garage.

Create cool spots by freezing hot-water bottles overnight, wrapping them in a towel or old pillow case and letting your guinea pigs choose to lie near them if they get too warm – or not, the choice is theirs.

ASK JAMES:
What do I do if I spot a problem with my pet?

Vets and vet nurses are always here to help! We are animal doctors but also animal dentists, surgeons, groomers and more! We are animal lovers ourselves and know how upsetting it can be when your pet is unwell. So try not to worry too much, because we're here to help 24/7!

POO DETECTIVE

Finally, did you know that guinea pigs also eat their own first poo? YUK! And they can poop a whopping 100 times a day!

DOLLY'S DOS AND DON'TS

☑ DO let them hide! Guinea pigs do not like open spaces!

☒ DON'T rush! Guinea pigs are naturally timid and will run away if you try to grab them. Start with tasty treat offerings and talk quietly to them, build up trust and wait for them to come to you.

☑ DO go to the ground! Humans are huge in comparison to guinea pigs, so get down to their level.

X DON'T be surprised if they offer you a kiss of love! If a guinea pig gently licks you, it is their way of saying they see you as one of their own, and then you really know you've cracked it!

✓ DO try a gentle head or chin stroke first. This is a great way to show your guinea pigs some love! NEVER stroke a guinea pig's fur in the 'opposite' direction – going against the fur is very unpleasant for a guinea pig's sensitive coat.

CHAPTER SIX

CHINCHILLAS

Sticking with rodents, chinchillas are fascinating little animals that have become an increasingly popular pet. With complex needs, a naturally shy character and a lifespan of up to TWENTY years, a chinchilla might not seem like the easiest pet to talk to! But in order to communicate with chinchillas, it helps to know a few key things.

HANDS OFF!: Chinchillas are quite nervous and don't really want to be handled that much, so they don't love lots of strokes or cuddles. They prefer human interaction with training and games (they can learn their names and learn to hop into a carrier!).

BATH TIME (IN SAND): Chinchillas need a daily sand bath in a tray of specialist chinchilla sand for twenty minutes a day. Never bath a chinchilla in water, as they quickly become too cold.

CHILL OUT: Their thick coat keeps them lovely and warm, but this also means chinchillas can quickly overheat in the summer. Keeping them cool and dry is key to their happiness. A cold slab of marble in their cage is a great option. They don't like wind and they don't like rain – which makes them an indoor pet.

HOUSEKEEPING: Chinchillas like to keep really clean – so make sure you clean their cage regularly and sieve their sand bath to remove any chinny-poos that might otherwise get buried or stuck to their coat.

SIGNS YOUR CHINCHILLA IS HAPPY

You can communicate with chinchillas by watching out for important clues in their body language. For example, happy chinchillas will show these signs:

- They will be alert and curious, choosing to move towards things to investigate.

- Their eyes will be big and bright.

- They will be active and agile.

Their coat will be healthy, soft, and non-greasy.

Chinchillas rarely bite — but they do occasionally nibble! This nibbling is a chinchilla's normal way of being inquisitive. It's NOT the same as biting, and although you can move your hand away, do not shriek or tell them off as this will stress them out.

SIGNS YOUR CHINCHILLA IS STRESSED OUT

Chinchillas that show these signs might be stressed out:

- They have patches of fur which drop out when handled.

- They chew their own fur, which can indicate boredom, stress or poor diet.

- They move around less, and crouch down with low ears and their head turned away.

- They hide more.

- They repeat certain movements over and over again (running in circles or back and forth).

- They have sores on the soles of their feet.

- They make a growling sound or show their teeth.

If your chinchilla is showing signs of stress, it might be that you need to adjust some of their daily routines or move their cage somewhere quieter. Either way, tell a grown-up and arrange for them to be checked by a vet.

HOW TO TALK TO YOUR CHINCHILLA

Chinchillas don't particularly like to be handled or cuddled, but there are many other ways we can communicate our love for them:

- Target practice: Train chinchillas to move towards a target like a cuddly toy. Start by showing the toy through the cage bars, and every time they come near, offer them a treat. Soon, they will recognise that moving TOWARDS the cuddly toy means they get a treat.

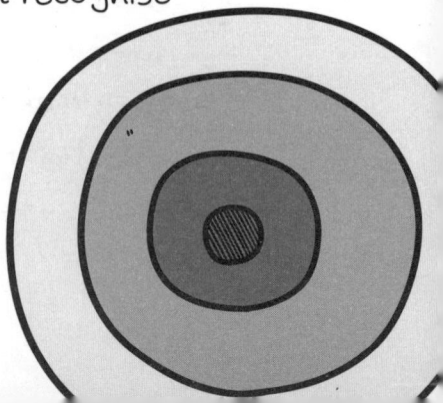

🐾 Enter the Chinchilla Olympics: Once they are settled and enjoying regular free exercise in whichever quiet room you have set up for them, you can upgrade this by setting up an agility course.

I'M GOING FOR GOLD!

🐾 Reward their behaviours to encourage your chinchillas to hop into a carrier case! You could even quietly say their name at the same time, and they will quickly realise that if you say their name and they hop in, they will get a treat!

ONE FINAL WORD OF WARNING!

A chinchilla that feels scared or threatened will DEFINITELY let you know in a very unpleasant way – they will rear up on their back legs and spray urine in the face of any perceived danger or threat!

DOLLY'S DOS AND DON'TS

✓ DO go super, super slow! It can take weeks (or even months) for your chinchillas to get used to your voice and build their confidence – be prepared to put time in to build that trust.

✗ DON'T overdo the cuddles! Chinchillas do not want to be handled lots.

✓ DO work with your chinchilla's natural curiosity. Always move very slowly around them.

X DON'T overdo it! Remember, if you do hold your chinchilla, keep handling times to a minimum and NEVER handle them roughly or they may shed their fur.

✓ DO think about games and training rather than cuddles and kisses. Training your chinchilla to hop into their carrier can be a useful skill when it comes to taking a trip to the vet or when it's time for them to return to their cages!

CHAPTER SEVEN

HAMSTERS AND GERBILS

In this chapter, I've brought hamsters and gerbils together! WOAH, STOP! They can't live together, but being of a similar size, they do share some similarities. However, they also have some VERY BIG differences. So let's take a look . . .

HAMSTERS
WHAT THEY DON'T WANT
DAYLIGHT

The bright sun is a hamster's arch enemy. They are nocturnal, which means they are active at night. And when I say active, I mean REALLY active! In the wild, a hamster will easily walk a mile every day!

IM A HAM-PIRE!

COMPANY

Hamsters are happy living on their own, doing their own thing and not caring what anyone else thinks of them! It might not sound that fun to us, but then we are not hamsters (although - you'd better just check that mirror once more to make sure! Nope? Phew!).

Trying to force a second hamster friend on them is cruel as it will very likely end up in a fight. So the golden rule, without exception, is to always keep them on their own.

(But don't worry - when it comes to humans, hamsters make an exception - they are happy to hang out with us!)

WHAT THEY DO WANT

BURROWING

Hamsters love to burrow and create tunnels. Some hamster cages come with all sorts of plastic tubes and tunnels that connect to each other, going up, down and round corners. These are fine, but hamsters aren't very good climbers! Most prefer to dig their own tunnels.

SPACE

If hamsters were people, they'd go for long strolls in the countryside with a lovely picnic. But since they're hamsters, we can't let them outside. So it's better to give them a large enclosure to roam in, with at least 25 cm of deep bedding so they can also dig down and make their own tunnels.

THE PET FILES

Hamsters can carry a surprisingly vast amount of food by cramming it into their cheek pouches (which also makes them look ridiculous and INCREDIBLY cute!). Their cheeks can fit the equivalent of us stuffing a fully inflated football into each side of our mouths!

HOW DO YOU DO THAT?

HOW TO HANDLE A HAMSTER

When we are wide awake, hamsters tend to be fast asleep! So when a hand dives into the hammy house, a hamster might go into self-defence mode and give you a little nippy bite! OUCH!

HAROLD!

Go steady and first of all, talk to them! You can even call your hamster by its name. Once they're fully awake, only then can you try cupping your hands together underneath their whole bodies to make the shape of a soup bowl and gently pick them up.

NOT TOO HOT, NOT TOO COLD, JUST RIGHT!

Hamsters are pretty sensitive to variations in temperature. In the hot summer, make sure

their enclosure isn't in direct sunlight or in a room that might become dangerously hot (such as a conservatory). But don't let them get too cool either. Make sure they're kept indoors – not in cold outbuildings or sheds.

ASK JAMES:
Should hamsters use plastic balls for exercise?

NOPE! They're actually pretty stressful for hamsters. Instead, **create a safe indoor enclosure with walls tall enough that they can't escape** and allow them some free-run exercise with loads of toys, obstacles and digging spots for them to explore or hide in.

GERBILS

If you crossed a mouse with a kangaroo that uses ultrasonic sounds like a whale, you would end up with something a bit like a gerbil!

There are over a hundred different species of gerbil, but the one we most commonly recognise in the world of pets is the Mongolian gerbil.

They are friendly, they don't bite (much!) and they don't even produce that much wee – which means they keep their homes nice and clean (less work for us!) and they don't smell much.

HELLO!

FAMILY FIRST

In the wild, gerbils live in large family groups. Dad gerbils will teach the babies digging skills and gather nesting materials from the sandy grassland regions where they live, and mum gerbils will show the babies what they can and can't eat.

Gerbils are expert diggers and will create a complex system of tunnels, with between ten and twenty exit and entry points for their group to live in. They can hear exceptionally well, and they can emit a kind of ultrasonic sound from their voice box that they use to communicate all sorts of messages to each other.

Sadly, we aren't able to hear what they're saying with our human ears! Which is a shame, as I'd love to know what gerbils chat about!

THE PET FILES

Gerbils can jump up to 30 cm from a standstill using their powerful back legs. So it's really important to always hold them near to the ground and be aware of their gerbil gymnastic skills!

Gerbils want three main things when we keep them as pets . . .

TO DIG

Gerbils need to live in a large glass tank with a wire mesh lid, filled with lots of bedding.

Gerbils want to dig tunnels for themselves, following their own gerbil rules and plans. Because of this, they need lots of space and a big, deep tank

FRIENDS

Gerbils like to chat. Even at gerbil-school they are allowed to talk all day long and they will even talk to us! If you ever hear a gerbil make a chirping sound towards you, that is their way of saying hello – try chatting back in a quiet, calm voice.

YOU FORGOT THE PUNCHLINE!

CHIRP CHIRP CHIRP

A same-sex pair (or more) will live happily together, but be careful introducing new gerbils into an established friendship group as this can result in a dangerous fight breaking out.

PEACE AND QUIET

Their ultrasonic sound system of hearing is super sensitive, which is why they really, really don't like other noises – so use your quiet voice.

THE PET FILES

Pet gerbils can be active day or night. When holding a gerbil, allow them to sniff your hand first, give them a gentle stroke, then cup your hand over their back and use your other hand underneath to support them. Finally, NEVER, EVER pick a gerbil up by its tail.

DOLLY'S DOS AND DON'TS

☑ DO keep hamsters on their own!

☒ DON'T forget hamsters can walk a mile in a day!

☑ DO allow hamsters to forage for their food – this helps keep them busy and makes them feel useful!

☒ DON'T raid their snack stash! Hamsters store food in their beds – it's part of their natural behaviour.

✓ DO keep gerbils with other gerbils –
they need friends around them.

✗ DON'T forget gerbils JUMP! So be very
careful handling them and always stay
close to the ground.

✓ DO stay quiet around gerbils and
watch what you say about them – they
can hear you very, very well!

✗ DON'T ever
grab a
gerbil by
its tail!

Now for one of my all-time favourite pets: RATS! Rats are curious, friendly, social, smart, very active and have bags and bags of personality – yet they have such an unfair reputation as being dirty, diseased and disgusting. Rats are incredibly clean and will groom themselves as often as cats do.

SO WHY IS THERE ALL THIS 'RAT HATE'?

It is true that wild rats may carry diseases that can spread to people, and I would NEVER try to befriend a wild rat. But our domestic rat species never come into contact with wild rats.

Of course, pet rats, like ALL pets, do have the potential to carry diseases – but by following some simple pet hygiene rules like hand washing

after handling and not kissing them or letting them lick our faces, we can reduce this risk right down.

RATS ARE SOCIAL

Like lots of the other rodents we have met, rats too need the company of other rats and can't be kept on their own. However, whilst rats like to live in a rat pack, most rats LOVE their humans equally as much!

WE'RE A RAT PACK!

Each rat has their own personality and will form strong bonds with other rats and with their human carer.

Rats are incredibly intelligent and can be trained to come when you say their name, complete an agility course, give a 'high five', solve puzzles and recognise the sounds and smells of different people. Some people believe rats are easily as smart as dogs, so I'd say whatever tricks a dog can do, a rat can do too!

THE PET FILES

To train your rat to come when called, start by offering a treat right in front of them. The moment they reach out with their front paws to take the treat, say their name out loud – just their name, keep things simple!

Repeat this for a few days, then try holding the treat an arm's length away from them. When they move towards your hand to take the treat, say their name!

Then try moving even further away and repeat. Eventually, they will come running whenever they hear their name being called because they know something good will happen!

Whilst rats don't like loud bangs, slamming doors, thumping music or loud voices, they do quite like to hear their own human's voice and watch what you are up to! For that reason, they like their cage to be somewhere quiet but also positioned so they can watch all the action.

To handle a rat, place one hand around their body behind their front legs and the other under their back legs, then lift them up, holding them close into your body.

Unlike most rodents, rats quite like to be carried around with you, so don't be surprised if they decide you are the perfect climbing frame to hitch a ride on. Perhaps that is why a group of rats is called a 'mischief'!

IMPORTANT NOTE: Rats like to scent mark everything, which is a polite way of saying they pee everywhere they go! Rudely, it also means they will probably pee on you. Rats often wee every few minutes when they are exploring a new place – so be ready with a tissue if you do let them climb all over you and, of course, wash your jumper and your hands afterwards!

ACRO-RAT-ICS

Rats are amazing at acrobatics and they
need at least one hour out of their cage
every day. Just make sure the room has been
suitably rat-proofed by covering exit points
and cables and removing houseplants.

In their cage, they will also
need somewhere to sleep.
Rats are nocturnal, although
they will be active in the
early evenings, which is the
best time to get them out for
handling.

Make sure they have a comfy nest box to sleep
in during the day, filled with some shredded
paper or hay.

THE PET FILES

Scientists have discovered that when rats are really happy, they giggle! Sadly, we can't hear such high frequencies, but scientists have likened the behaviour to us laughing with our friends! Forget the dad jokes, I need to start telling rat jokes!

How can you tell when a rat's done the housework?

Because they leave the place SQUEAKY CLEAN!

HAHA HA HA!

SIGNS YOUR RAT IS A BIT STRESSED OUT

Friendly, curious, with a nice smooth coat, healthy bright eyes and a friendly character: these are all signs your rat is in a good mood and happy.

There are a few signs to watch out for, though, that might suggest your rat isn't as happy as they could be:

- Rats are prone to chest infections, so listen for wheezy breathing or sneezing and look out for runny noses or eyes.

- A rat that doesn't want to play or come to greet you is a sign that something is wrong.

- Look out for any lumps and bumps that may appear on their body.

- Rats that are unhappy can produce a reddy-brown liquid around their eyes and nostrils – this can make them look like they're having a nosebleed, but usually it is a pigment called porphyrin. This is not blood, but it is a sign your rat is in pain or stressed and should be checked out by a vet.

GRAB YOUR SWIMMERS!

OK – one final way to talk with rats is to offer them the opportunity to go for a quick paddle! Some rats are really good swimmers (but that doesn't mean all rats want to go swimming). Try filling a shallow tray with some room-temperature water, place your rat nearby and see whether they choose to go for a paddle. You may even see them having a full wash and splash about!

DOLLYS DOS AND DON'TS

✓ DO keep a rat pack – they need friends to play and form strong bonds with.

✗ DON'T let them get bored! A bored rat is a stressed rat. They need lots of toys, a big cage and lots of playtime, and they will LOVE learning new tricks with you.

✓ DO let them search for their food – sprinkle their food around the cage instead of using a bowl. This is an easy way to leave them with an activity if you need to pop out.

X DON'T forget they need their sleep! Rats like to sleep in the day, so make sure you give them lots of time to rest in and amongst all the playing.

✓ DO expect to become best friends! Rats love their humans as much as we love them, so the more time you can spend with them, the happier they will be.

CHAPTER NINE

FISH

Did you know, a few minutes a day spent observing fish swim around in their tank has been proven to improve our mood, reduce anxiety and help boost our mental health? That's pretty 'fin-tastic' if you ask me!

HOW TO TALK TO YOUR FISH

Fish communicate with each other in lots of ways – motion sensors, electrical impulses, and some can even glow with light called bioluminescence. Scientists have recently discovered that different species of fish even communicate by making sounds: from grunts, clicks and pops to frantic humming. Sardines even fart at each other as a way of talking! HOW GROSS IS THAT?!

PRRRP!

BAP!

PRAAP

But is it possible for us to communicate with our pet fish? The answer is YES!

Despite what people may say, science shows that fish have quite impressive memories – goldfish can remember where they get fed, can remember when they have done something and been rewarded and can recognise other goldfish friends even after they have been separated.

$$E = M^{SEA^2}$$

This all proves that fish are intelligent, sensitive beings that deserve our respect and care, the same as all animals do.

Fish can hear sounds outside their tank – so may even start to recognise their owner's voice. They also have something called a 'lateral line' along their bodies – this helps to pick up vibrations. It is really important to **NEVER tap or bang on your fish tank** – or play loud, thumping music, as they will feel the vibrations through the water, and it's seriously stressful for them.

Gentle vibrations, though, can be helpful to your fish. They can recognise certain patterns or behaviours to work out what's going on around their tank. For example – you might notice they all come swimming to the surface when you're about to feed them, even before the food has touched the water!

This isn't because they see, hear or smell the food – they have felt the vibrations of you walking towards the tank! They know it's dinner time!

The safest way to talk to your fish is through actions, not words. Food is a big deal for fish. 'A hungry fish is a healthy fish!'

We want to keep the water in their tank as clean as possible – so I don't recommend any fish games where you have to put your hands or toys in the water. Instead, use plants to create hiding places and try offering different types of food to keep their interest – some fish prefer pellets that sink to the bottom, others like food that floats on the surface and almost every freshwater fish will enjoy a tasty snack of frozen bloodworms!

ASK JAMES:
Why do my fish always hide away so I can't see them?

Well, even pet fish are scared that something will eat them — whether that's a bigger fish or a bird flying overhead. Giving your fish more plants, more bridges, more rocks and more places for them to escape to will help them feel SOOOO much more confident. In fact, the more places they have to hide, the more likely you will see them swimming in the open water! You're now talking in fish language!

THE PET FILES

Studies show that fish have feelings, the same as a dog or cat might. They can experience fear, pain and distress, but also positive emotions such as joy and pleasure. Fish can also be quite playful and mischievous – chasing and riding the bubble streams in their tanks and living in a social structure of friends, much like we do! Fish want to live in perfect harmony with the water around them – a properly nurtured fish tank becomes a self-contained ecosystem all of its own, in which your fish will thrive. On the other hand, a neglected tank that is not properly cared for will quickly become a green soup of fish poo and rotting food – absolutely no one wants that!

WHICH FISH?

To understand what fish need, we first need to know which different types of fish we can look after as pets.

First up – we'll head to the ocean. If you have ever watched nature documentaries about coral reefs, they often feature brightly coloured 'tropical marine' fish. Looking after these fish requires a deep understanding of water chemistry, salt levels, pH levels and all the complexities that come with trying to recreate a mini ocean in your front room!

OOH – HIDDEN TREASURE!

Closer to home, the 'cold-water marine' fish refers to pretty much anything you'd find on UK shores, from John O'Groats to Land's End. The best way to get up close and personal with these guys is to head out to the rockpools along our UK coastline and watch them in their natural environment (preferably with an ice cream at the same time – mine's a 99, thanks!).

Most people, though, keep freshwater fish. These can be cold-water fish such as goldfish in a tank or Koi Carp in a pond – or they can be tropical aquarium species such as guppies and mollies, found living wild in places such as Central or South America and the Amazon basin.

WHAT DO THEY NEED?
WATER

The water we drink from the tap contains chemicals to make it safe for us, but those chemicals are very damaging to pet fish. Tap water needs a special liquid conditioner from the pet shop to be added, to neutralise any harmful chemicals before it comes into contact with fish tanks.

WARM OR COLD

Tropical fish like warm water, so they will need a water heater in the tank, set to a specific level to keep the fish at the correct water temperature.

HOUSEKEEPING

We need to use an electric water filter to keep everything clean. The main purpose of this is to remove the fish poo, any uneaten food and some of the harmful toxins in the tank.

OXYGEN

Some tanks will require an oxygen pump – this pushes air bubbles through the water to keep the tank full of life, giving oxygen for the fish to extract through their gills. As a general rule, the best tanks are those with a large surface area, like rectangular aquariums.

ASK JAMES:
How else can I keep the tank water clean?

In the wild, the water a fish lives in is constantly refreshed either by rain or as the water moves along the river. You need to replicate this in your fish tank by replacing 30% of the tank water with fresh water once a week to help keep the tank clean and healthy. NEVER completely empty and replace all the water in one go — this is too big a shock to your fish and can ruin all your hard work to build up the right bacteria balance in your tank.

WHERE'S HOME FOR YOUR FISH?

Think carefully about where to position your tank – you won't be able to move it once it's full. It is also important not to place your tank on a windowsill or in direct sunlight, as this can affect the water temperature and encourage an overgrowth of algae.

ASK JAMES:
Do fish sleep?

Fish like to rest at night like we do, so have the tank lights on in the day and off at night. You can even use a timer so you don't have to remember to keep switching them on and off!

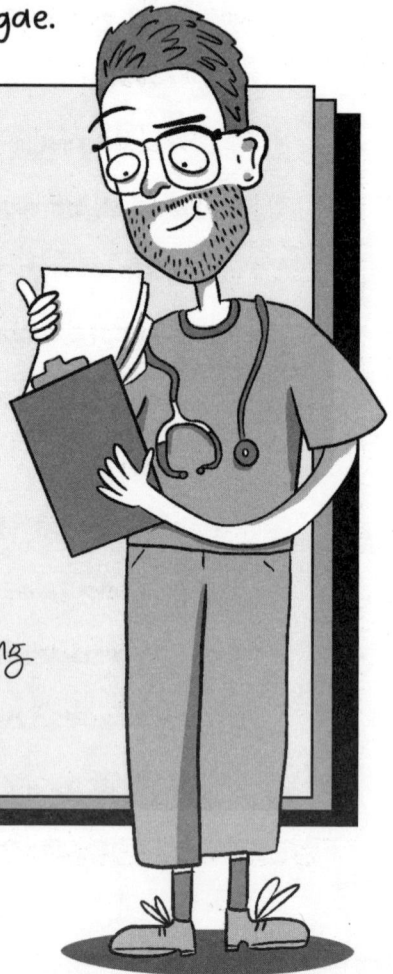

DOLLY'S DOS AND DON'TS

DO put lots of time into researching which type of fish you want to keep, how big they will grow and which fish can live together.

DON'T forget to let your tank establish before you add any live fish.

DO place your tank on a solid surface, out of direct sunlight.

DON'T bang, tap or knock on the tank – this is super stressful.

DO provide lots of plants and places to hide – the more places they have to hide, the more comfortable they will feel.

WARNING!
IF YOU'RE NOT A FAN OF CREEPY-CRAWLIES
DO NOT ENTER!

Lots of bugs make **GREAT PETS!** Their tank becomes a mini rainforest or jungle in your room with insects and critters of all shapes and sizes, and the best part is they are often pretty easy to look after! Creepy-crawlies are the masters of camouflage, so grab your magnifying glass and keep your eyes peeled as we head into the undergrowth and find out what insects want . . . *(JUST WATCH OUT FOR THE SPIDER-WEBS!)*

STICK INSECTS

Hmmm, the name is possibly a bit of a giveaway here – but the coolest thing about stick insects is their incredible camouflage skill. As you can probably guess, to avoid becoming a tasty snack for a passing bird, the 3,000 or so different species of stick insects have all evolved to look just like . . . sticks! They live on vegetation and make great pets, as most are very easy to look after.

Can you spot me!

MEET THE STICKS

Stick insects are the LONGEST INSECTS IN THE WORLD (which makes sense, as their job is to mimic a stick!). Most tend to be green, brown or yellow, some have thorny spikes over their twig bodies to look like brambles, and

others even have wings! The most common species available in the UK is the Indian stick insect – but others come in all sorts of different leaf shapes and stick sizes!

STICK INSECTS NEED:

- An enclosed tank to live in with air holes for ventilation, with lots of space to crawl out of their skins when they moult

- To be kept warm — they are tropical insects, after all! (Just make sure to keep them out of direct sunlight or cold draughts)

- Brambles, privet, hawthorn, or rose leaves to munch on. Some stick insect species will only eat specific vegetation so it is always worth checking, but most of the stick insects available in pet shops will thrive on these plants

HOW TO HANDLE YOUR STICKIES

If you want to pick up a stick insect, instead of grabbing them from above – which is really stressful for them because you might look like a predator – hold your palm out flat and allow them to walk on to your hand or gently encourage them to hitch a ride on the soft bristles of a paintbrush.

The most important thing to remember when handling your stickies is how fragile they are. As a last resort, when they think their life is in danger, they will detach a leg. As a result, it is important to never pick them up by a leg or 'pull' them away from their branch. Though, if they do accidentally get into a sticky situation and lose a leg, these phenomenal phasmids will grow back a new one when they next shed their skin. WOW!

GIANT AFRICAN LAND SNAILS

As large as a human fist and weighing the same as one to two tins of baked beans, these are the largest land snails on the planet.

They live in damp areas of Africa, grow up to 20 cm and can live for eight or nine years. But what else do these mammoth molluscs want from us to help them thrive as pets?

A NICE WARM BED OF SOIL!

Snails can slime their way out of most enclosures, so a sturdy glass or plastic tank is essential – with a lid and air holes for ventilation. They like it a little warmer than our typical homes, so it is a good idea to provide an external heat mat under the tank set to 20–25 degrees Celsius on the thermometer.

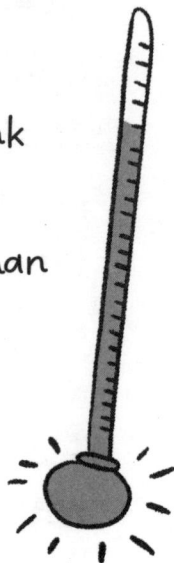

They also like it humid, so we have to mist the tank with fresh water once or twice every day. The tanks also need a deep bed – which can be a mix of peat-free compost, leaf litter and moss – so that it won't dry out too quickly or lose too much heat. Avoid bark or wood chips, sand or sawdust, and placing rocks or anything metal, ceramic or sharp in their enclosure – they're too sharp for snails.

GIMME THAT DECAY . . .

Giant African land snails are detritivores – **THIS MEANS THEY EAT DECAYING MATTER!** Anything too fresh and they will turn one of their FOUR little snail noses up at it. That's right – four noses! No wonder they have such a super sense of smell.

HANDLING

It's true that your snail is never going to outrun you so they're pretty easy to catch – but still, try not to handle your snails for too long or too often. If you do need to lift them out of their tank for any reason, DO NOT pick them up by the shell! Where their shell meets the body is a particularly sensitive area and any pressure here can hurt them – *OUCH!* Instead, the best way is to wet your hands with water and slide a finger underneath

their body, then slide your whole hand under and use your other hand to gently support them. Snails are nocturnal, so they may be easier to handle in the evenings. You can talk to them in a quiet voice, call their name and reward them with some food – but . . . you might be waiting a **LONG TIME** for any response – there's a reason they call it 'snail's pace' because snails move very, very slowly!

IMPORTANT NOTE: It is important to ALWAYS wash your hands thoroughly after handling your snail and never kiss the snail shell, as they may carry certain bacteria such as salmonella, which can make you poorly.

MADAGASCAN HISSING COCKROACH

Yep, you heard me right! One of the largest cockroaches on the PLANET – and some people keep them as PETS! 'WHAT?' I hear you shriek – but don't rock your roaches just yet, because once you've heard a bit more about them, you too might become a cockroach convert!

As their name suggests, they are from the island of Madagascar and will make a loud 'hissing' sound through 'spiracles' (respiratory openings on their abdomen) to scare off predators or when two males fight.

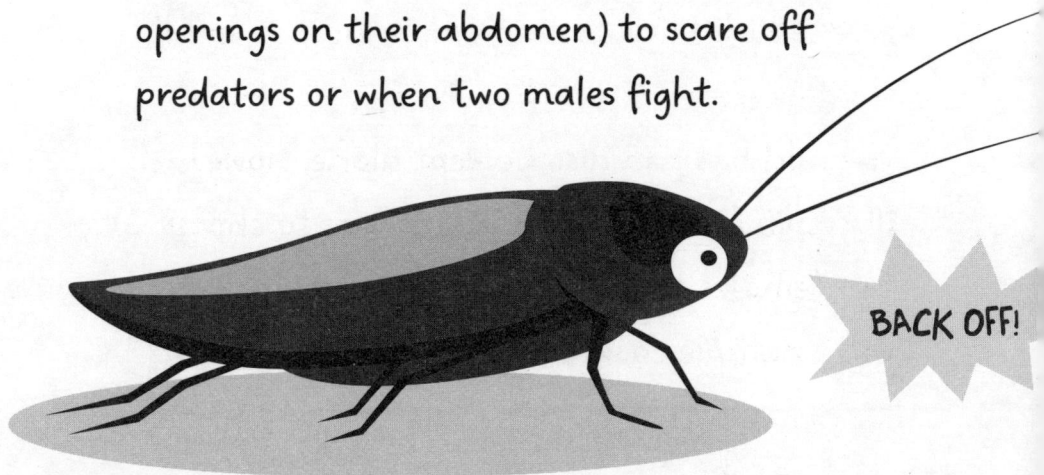

BACK OFF!

180

Towards humans, they are docile, don't mind being handled and can't bite! Earning themselves *THREE BIG GOLD PET-STARS!*

HOUSING

Cockroaches need a glass or plastic tank with a securely fitting lid. They can live on most types of bedding, from coir (which comes from coconut shells) and wood shavings to soil and sand. Wood bark can be used to create hiding places, and they need a small, shallow water bowl. They live in colonies in the wild but can also be kept alone. However, if keeping more than one, it is wise to choose two females or there is a risk you could end up with multiple cockroaches!

HOW TO TALK TO YOUR COCKROACH

The most important thing is to NOT make any hissing sounds! Instead, use quiet voices and chat away so they can hear your voice, and reward them with tasty food. If you want to talk in extra 'cockroach friendly' ways, try to avoid saying any words with an 'S' sound – as they might mistake that for hissing!

BANNED WORDS!
- SAUSAGES
- SARDINES
- SATSUMAS
- SING-SONG

TARANTULA

These guys will either give you the creeps and you'll throw this book across the room just at the **VERY MENTION OF THE 'T' WORD AND THEIR BIG HAIRY EIGHT LEGS!** Aaaaaghhh! OR you'll be instantly fascinated by these giants of the spider world, in which case, let's have a good look at what tarantulas need, because you might be surprised at how they actually want for very little:

- A safe, secure tank or enclosure to call home

- Warmth from a heat mat

- Humidity at the right level for the species

Ventilation — yes, they need warm, humid air — but never stagnant or stale air, and the tank should not smell mouldy

Somewhere to hide — they need a shelter

Suitable bedding in the base of the tank

Regular meals of small insects once or twice a week

Tarantulas only poo out very tiny white parcels of spider poo, so they don't need to be cleaned out like other pets do. However, uneaten food and leftovers should be removed after twenty-four hours.

HANDLING

Despite what you might see online, tarantulas should NOT BE HANDLED! They are fascinating creatures and can make for very interesting pets without needing a huge amount from us, but this is a pet to observe like you might do fish in a fish tank.

Even docile species can suddenly turn defensive if they feel threatened and they have FANGS THAT CAN EASILY PIERCE HUMAN SKIN.

They can scrape special hairs from their backs and legs and flick them into the eyes, nose and face of any animal they deem to be a threat (which could include you!). This can cause severe itchiness and damage – so it is

a good idea to wear goggles and gloves, keep them away from your face and always wash your hands after handling anything in their tank, as the hairs can be left around the tank too.

Perhaps the biggest danger with handling is actually to them! Tarantulas can suddenly decide to run, and if you accidentally drop them – even just from knee height – it can seriously hurt their delicate bodies.

HOW TO TALK TO YOUR TARANTULA

Tarantulas are definitely not a pet to try and cuddle! They are best observed from a distance. But that doesn't mean we can't talk to them. Tarantulas are 'sit and wait' predators, meaning they wait for food to

come to them, and we can help them out! They **HATE** loud bangs and strong vibrations – these are danger signs to a tarantula and will make them run into their burrow and hide away. However, small scuttery vibrations could mean a tasty snack is walking by – this makes them come out from their dens in hope of dinner time. Each time you place some food near the burrow, try gently tapping the table about 10 cm away from the tank. This tells them 'dinner is served' – you are now your tarantula's butler!

DOLLY'S DOS AND DON'TS

X DON'T forget about the bugs! Insects and critters can make great pets!

X DON'T ever grab an insect from above – the shadow and shape of your hand hovering above them will look like a predator.

✓ DO be careful of the sounds you make in front of a cockroach – stay quiet and avoid any words beginning with 'S'!

X DON'T forget to count your stick insects – they are experts at camouflage!

✓ DO always remember to tell your tarantula when their dinner is ready!

CHAPTER ELEVEN

REPTILES

Reptiles come in all different shapes and sizes –
from snakes and turtles to lizards and more.
They've been around for a VERY long time –
the first ones evolving around 315 MILLION
YEARS AGO.

WE'VE STILL GOT IT!

They are known for having scales on their
bodies, instead of hair or feathers like
mammals and birds.

Lots of reptiles are sadly endangered and
their homes are under threat, mostly from

human beings. It is really important we help to conserve wild reptiles by making sure we only keep pet reptiles that have been bred in captivity.

For the ones that are available as pets, though, it's important to understand how to talk to them.

WHAT ARE THEY TRYING TO SAY?

LET'S CRACK THE CASE!

Reptiles don't use facial expressions or their voices to show their feelings. We need to put our pet detective caps on to spot clues as to how a reptile is feeling and then figure out how to talk to them.

191

By studying
everything a reptile
does in the wild, we can
compare that information
to how they are behaving as
pets. This allows us to keep an eye
out for any 'stress' signals. Certain
body movements can also give a clear
sign of a reptile's mood. GETTING TO
KNOW WHAT'S 'NORMAL' IS REALLY
IMPORTANT.

PUTTING THE 'S' IN SNAKE:

When a snake curls the front part of
its body into a tight 'S' shape – like a
coiled spring – this is a sign that they
are about to 'strike' forward and bite. If
they strike towards their dinner – that's
normal. If there is no food around and

they make this shape towards their owner – it is a warning sign to keep your distance!

GROW A BEARD: Bearded dragons, or 'beardies', are so-called due to the skin under their chin that 'puffs' out when they feel stressed, making it look like a big beard!

If a beardie is repeatedly showing this behaviour, it's because something is seriously stressing them out. If they suddenly hiss at the same time, this is a warning sign that they are about to bite! Thankfully, most beardies are very friendly towards people. PHEW.

GETTING BITTEN BY A REAL-LIFE DRAGON? WOAH – NO THANK YOU!

STICK YOUR TONGUE OUT: Snakes and lizards can smell and taste chemicals in the air that tell them all about their environment – especially whether or not there is some potential food lurking nearby. Their famous 'forked' tongue allows them to pick up maximum smell particles! So if a snake is flicking its tongue, it's a sign they are a happy snake interested in the world around them.

NOD ALONG: A nodding head doesn't mean your bearded dragon agrees with everything you say! Instead, it's a sign they may be feeling stressed – perhaps they've been handled a bit too much that day, and it's their way of asking for a break and saying they need some time alone, back in their vivarium (this is the name for the enclosure pet reptiles are kept in).

MULTICOLOUR MOODS:

Chameleons are famous for being able to change the colour of their skin to reflect their mood. Scientists have discovered special nanocrystals within their skin cells that push closer together when the chameleon is relaxed, which makes the skin appear blue and green. When they are excited, the nanocrystals move further apart – which makes the skin appear red and yellow! YOU CAN LITERALLY READ THEIR MOOD BY WHAT COLOUR THEY ARE!

Bearded dragons are also able to change colour – they'll turn black when they feel too cold or they're stressed – perhaps because of loud noises, other pets or being handled too much.

If you see a colour change in a reptile, as fascinating as it is – **THE FIRST QUESTION YOU MUST ASK IS: WHY?** You can talk to them by providing a more natural environment, keeping noise levels down, perhaps reducing the amount of time they are handled and by keeping other pets well away from their tank.

SNAIL'S PACE WINS THE RACE: Tortoises may move slowly, but that doesn't stop them from being super curious! They love to explore, forage, dig, climb and bask in the sun. They'll also follow their owners and can even learn their names! A happy tortoise is one that is interested in the world around it.

C'MON, SPIKES!

ASK JAMES
Why do some lizards 'wave'?

Some lizards seem to 'wave' at their humans! They raise one arm into the air and rotate their 'hands' — exactly the same way we would. Waving is usually their way of saying, 'I mean no harm!' It is not necessarily a stress sign unless they also run away into a hiding place.

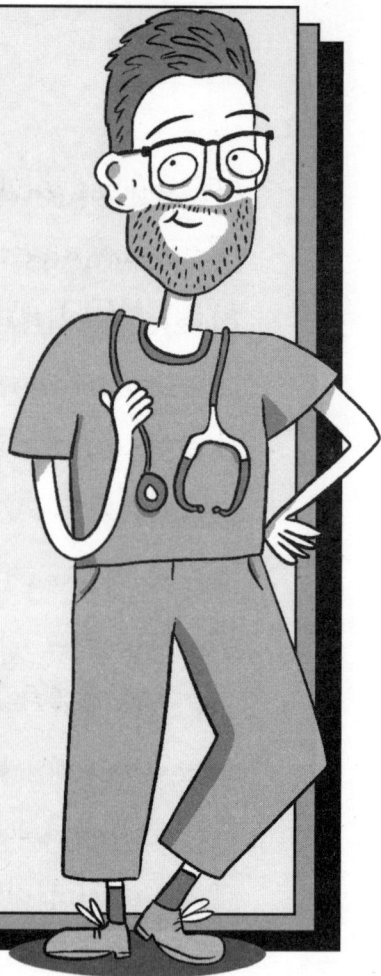

HOW TO TALK BACK

The best way to talk to wild animals is to stay very quiet and watch them from a distance, so the same applies to lots of pet reptiles too. But for certain pet reptiles, a short amount

of gentle handling can help them bond with their humans – talking to reptiles through touch can help them to realise we are not a threat. So here are my top tips . . .

LIZARDS

Before trying to handle any lizard, check what species it is. Some lizards with very delicate skin should not be handled unless necessary. Geckos may shed their tails if they feel scared, whilst poorly reptiles may have soft bones that can break easily.

Some lizards are naturally aggressive – such as the green iguana with its very powerful tail, which is able to swing round and whip hard – LOOK

OUT! Others, such as bearded dragons, are known for their calm and friendly personalities and may not mind being held.

🌱 Many beardies quite enjoy having human contact as they know it's an opportunity to absorb (or steal!) some of our body heat!

🌱 An open hand hovering over the top of a lizard will make them PANIC, RUN and HIDE! Why? Because it looks suspiciously like an eagle's claw swooping down to grab them. Instead – talk to them to let them know you're there, move slowly, hold your flat palm in front of them and gently slide it under their belly. Use the other hand to gently support the tail and bottom. Never lift a lizard by the head or tail or turn them on their backs, and don't squeeze or 'cuddle' them – instead just support them and watch out for any stress signals.

SNAKES

Snakes have two main defence mechanisms – bite or squeeeeeze! ALWAYS check the species of snake first. Venomous snakes should NEVER be handled, and large constrictor snakes need at least two people to handle them. Others, such as corn snakes, don't appear to mind being handled gently and don't tend to bite.

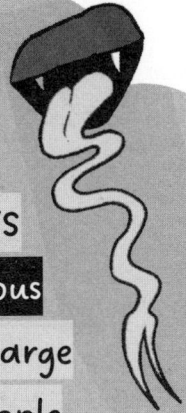

Corn snakes can be picked up gently by holding the middle part of their body with one hand and supporting their weight with your other. Never lift a snake by its tail or head. Snakes are very muscular and like to slither! Be ready to allow them to move from arm to arm, curling and uncurling, but never allow them to fully wrap around your arm and NEVER wear them around your neck. Snakes are snakes, not scarves!

Always feed your snake outside of their vivarium, otherwise they learn to expect food every time the door opens and may mistake your hand for a tasty snack! Woops!

TORTOISES

Most tortoises are happy to be gently lifted and moved, but it is important to keep them low to the ground. Tortoises don't breathe (well, not in the way we do anyway)! They draw air into their lungs through their noses by moving their arms, legs and neck in and out. That's why it's important to only hold a tortoise by its shell, as though you're holding a hamburger, and NEVER hold on to their limbs.

With all reptiles, keep handling times to a set limit each day and remember not to keep them away from their heat source for too long. NEVER handle a snake or lizard that is shedding its skin and NEVER in the two days after they have eaten, as this can interrupt their digestion, causing them to vomit. Finally, ALWAYS WASH YOUR HANDS before and after handling reptiles.

DRAGONS TO DINOSAURS, WHAT DO REPTILES WANT?

One of the best ways we can talk to reptiles is to copy, as closely as possible, the same life they would have in the wild. Reptiles are challenging pets to look after properly as their natural habitat may be in a completely different climate to ours, in a different country or even continent!

They need a safe vivarium suitable for their size. Snakes, for example, need to stretch their LONG BODIES out in full, and don't forget, some reptiles can grow VERY BIG, VERY QUICK!

If a lizard likes to burrow, they'll need the right ground to safely dig. A tortoise needs far more than to be left out in a garden, and if a snake prefers to hang out in trees, they'll need branches to climb up.

Finally, all reptiles want the choice to hide away from time to time in covered den areas to feel safe.

Here is what ALL reptiles need to thrive as pets . . .

MAKE IT BRIGHT AND RIGHT

Different reptiles need their own correct spectrum of ultraviolet light. This means fitting a special bulb in their home that emits the correct type of light for each species. This is important, as light is essential for reptiles to properly absorb nutrients, vitamins and calcium from their food and to keep their bones, skeletons and shell healthy.

On a nice sunny day, tortoises and bearded dragons often love a little trip outside! Just make sure they can't escape and have access to shade and water. Never force a reptile to do something they don't want to do and make sure they always have the choice to return to their preferred spot.

SEEK THE HEAT

Reptiles are 'ectothermic' – which means they use heat from their surroundings to warm themselves up or cool down. They can't survive the cold – this is why we don't find wild reptiles in places like the Antarctic! Keeping warm is essential for digestion, for movement and to lay eggs.

HERE COMES THE RAIN

How 'damp' the air is – humidity – also affects how happy reptiles are. Terrapins like water to swim in, but they also like to dry out in their basking zones. Some lizards and snakes, however, might prefer their home to be a lot drier – which helps prevent breathing or

skin problems. Chameleons like a night-time fog and will drink water droplets sprayed on to the leaves in their vivariums. **ALL REPTILES ARE DIFFERENT!**

DINNER TIME!

Feeding the right diet is also very important. A lot of reptiles will eat less often than mammals, so it is important to keep a diary of exactly what and when they eat. In the wild, snakes eat small mammals and birds, whereas tortoises and lizards may only eat plants or a mixture of plants and insects.

We do not feed live prey, other than insects, to reptiles in captivity as this is not fair on the animals and the snake could get injured or bitten. Instead, their food can be bought frozen. If you are not comfortable with the

idea of feeding a reptile the correct diet in captivity, they may not be the right pet for you.

WHAT'S FOR DINNER TONIGHT?

BARGAIN

THE PET FILES

A reptile's favourite place to poo is . . . wait for it . . . IN THE BATH! YUCK! A shallow, warm bath allows reptiles to drink and absorb the water, which in turn hydrates them and hey presto – poo starts moving through their tummies!

DOLLY'S DOS AND DON'TS

✓ DO research pet reptiles fully before thinking about caring for one. These are complicated animals to look after, and many suffer from being kept in the wrong conditions.

✓ DO only buy captive-bred reptiles and be aware some tortoises should have special paperwork.

✗ DON'T grab lizards from above – they will think you are a predator!

✓ DO feed the right diet for your species of reptile and provide them with the correct house, light, temperature and humidity.

DID YOU KNOW THAT HORSES SHARE MANY SIMILARITIES WITH RABBITS?

Well, it's true. They both need lots of fibre to help digest their food. They both have teeth that never stop growing. They are both unable to breathe through their mouths **AND** they are both unable to vomit.

Horses are not simply giant rabbits, though! (Thank goodness – imagine if a horse could hop like a bunny up into the air. BOING!)

Horses are members of the 'equine' family — that's a scientific term that covers ponies, donkeys and zebras too.

Members of the equine family are special. For one thing, they don't have hands or paws! Instead, the front legs of equine animals developed as the equivalent to our middle fingers, and the back leg as the equivalent to our middle toes. **THAT MEANS THAT A HOOF IS REALLY JUST ONE HUGE FINGER OR TOENAIL.**

This is why we take such special care of horses' feet and why they have regular visits from the farrier. A farrier is a person who cuts and shapes their hooves and fits metal horseshoes for extra protection. Whether you are desperate to have a horse of your own or find them **WOAH, WAY TOO BIG** — everyone can at least

appreciate the strength, power and magic of horses. (Oh, and speaking of magic, DID YOU KNOW THAT UNICORNS ARE REAL? More on that later . . .)

HOW TO TALK TO A HORSE

Horses, ponies and donkeys are very sensitive animals with lots of complex feelings. We have to understand them before we get close to them, for our safety and theirs.

Horses can 'spook' or 'jump' easily. This could be because of a passing car or even a plastic bag blowing in the wind. Their response is usually to startle, turn and run. When approaching a horse, always ensure there is nothing on your clothes or around you that could make a sudden noise, has flashing

lights or flaps in the wind. NEVER SHRIEK, CLAP OR RUN TOWARDS A HORSE! Here's how I say hello to a horse:

- Ask the owner or rider: Not all horses are friendly towards strangers, and some may be deep in concentration or being trained. Others might love all the attention in the world! If it's a horse I don't know, the safest (and most polite) place to start is to ask the person in charge.

- If they say it's OK: Walk towards the FRONT end (never approach a horse from behind) and talk in a calm, quiet voice. Say hello or even ask how their day was. It doesn't matter WHAT I'm saying as long as I talk in a calm, low voice. Horses have excellent hearing, and by chatting away to them, I'm letting them know exactly where I am at all times.

LET THEM DECIDE: If they choose to move away, I stop and let them. That is their way of saying, 'Not today, thanks!' and I respect that. However, if they lean their head to me, point their ears forward, relax their muzzle and even give me a gentle nudge with their nose, I know the horse is saying hello back and I might give them a gentle stroke down their neck!

WHERE DO WE STAND WITH HORSES?

Horses cannot see immediately in front of them OR directly behind them – these zones are called 'BLIND SPOTS'.

They could accidentally run you over if you walk right in front of them, or kick if you surprise them from behind.

Instead, always stand on the LEFT side of a horse (called the 'near side'), halfway between the horse's head and its shoulder. If you're standing still, point your feet and body towards the horse so you can make eye contact. This allows you to keep an eye on their body language and, importantly, they can see you too! NEVER turn your back on a horse – it only takes a split second for a horse to spook!

HOW TO READ HORSE BODY LANGUAGE

Horses neigh, whinny, nicker, snort, squeal, sigh, groan and blow! However, to understand a horse's mood, we have to look at their whole-body language. Horses and ponies can feel a range of positive and negative emotions.

Horses are powerful animals, so the more we can read the clues about how they feel, the safer and happier we can all be around them.

HOW TO SPOT A HAPPY HORSE

Look for a relaxed body that moves slowly. They have their ears pointed forward towards you and their muzzle will be relaxed. Their eyes are open but not wide and their head will be held at its normal height.

I'M HAPPY TO SEE YOU!

HOW TO SPOT A DOZING HORSE

If a horse is standing still with its head slightly lowered, eyes half shut, ears pointing sideways and muzzle relaxed with the lower lip dangling and floppy – this horse is very likely having a snooze!

As with all pets we've met, no animal likes to be suddenly woken up – so don't disturb this horse as you may accidentally frighten them!

HOW TO SPOT A SCARED HORSE

Scared or worried horses will lean back or even step backwards, have their head held high and ears pointing backwards, with their muzzle tense and nostrils wide open.
Their eyes will be wide open and possibly looking directly at whatever is scaring them, making the whites of their eyes show.

This horse is scared and may turn to run away or choose to defend itself, so DO NOT approach, and instead inform a grown-up.

HOW TO SPOT AN ANGRY HORSE

Horses have three options when they feel under attack – stand and fight, run away or freeze on the spot.

A horse that chooses to fight may rear (which means to stand up on their back legs and kick forward with their front legs) or kick out (they will 'jump' one or both back legs off the ground and throw a backwards kick), or they may even bite.

These can all lead to serious injury, so it is especially important to never approach an angry horse.

A horse that is warning you to stay away will have their ears pinned tightly backwards and may move their head to look directly at you. The head will be held high, the whites of their eyes will show and they may even lunge towards you with their mouth open and teeth showing.

MORE THAN JUST A PONY TAIL

An equine tail works as an excellent built-in fly swatter in the summer months, but beyond keeping bothersome bluebottles at bay, what else can we tell from a pony tail?

TAIL HELD HIGH

If the tail seems to arch higher than the horse's back and bottom, it's usually a sign they are excited. They're often a bit worked up, fidgety and about to gallop off or just go a bit bonkers! It's not necessarily an angry sign, but they can be a bit unpredictable.

Experienced riders may talk calmly in a reassuring voice to calm them down, but if it's a horse you don't know, it's better to keep a safe distance and watch from behind a fence.

TAIL CLAMPED DOWN

This is usually a sign a horse is feeling a bit scared or worried, or they may even be in pain.

An experienced rider might choose to reassure them or look for reasons why they are feeling uncomfortable, but if this is a horse you don't know, it's best to keep your distance and ask a grown-up to help.

SWISHING

Slow tail swishing from side to side whilst they are out grazing grass in the paddock is probably just a way to swat some flies. But a firm swish from side to side or up and down (like someone raising and banging their fist on a table) is a sign the horse is angry or upset and may be about to kick,

SO STAND WELL BACK!

HORSE CARE

In the wild, horses live in large family herds and spend most of the day with their head down munching on grass. Having lots of friends around means they can work as a team, and whilst one horse is grazing, another can be keeping an eye out for any predators.

Our pet horses may not need to look out for predators as they do in the wild, but they still like the company of living as a herd.

Wild horses will walk for hours each day, and so our pet horses also need lots of exercise too. As long as they can shelter from the sun, wind and rain, most horses are happiest being outside in the fresh air. They have different types of movement – walk, trot, canter and the fastest, the GALLOP! Woah, wait for

MEEEEEE!

GIDDY-UP!

Horses need a comfortable stable to keep them safe overnight or when they need to recover from being poorly. However, being alone in a stable can make horses feel lonely. Some people put safe plastic mirrors on the wall so they can choose to take a quick look at themselves from time to time and think they're not alone. AWWWW, CUTE!

223

A stable needs to be kept free of cobwebs and dust, be well ventilated and have super-clean bedding. Horses need lots of 'tack' or equipment – a properly fitted saddle, bridle, head halters, brushes and waterproof coats or 'rugs'. They may need extra protection from the flies and midges in the warmer months and need to be groomed daily.

They also need regular visits from the farrier to keep their hooves in good shape, the dentist to keep a check on those pearly whites and the vet to help keep them healthy!

DONKEYS ARE DIFFERENT

Donkeys are one of my favourite animals on the planet – and for this reason, they are getting their own special mention here!

Donkeys are **HIGHLY EMOTIONAL** and **INTELLIGENT ANIMALS** – they form deep, loving friendships with other donkeys – 'donkey soulmates' – and for this reason a donkey should never, ever be kept on its own.

Donkeys don't 'spook' or 'jump' like horses do. When they are scared, they don't tend to 'startle' and run but instead freeze on the spot. Often this 'freeze-on-the-spot' reaction gets mistaken for stubbornness.

DONKEYS ARE NOT STUBBORN. If a donkey suddenly stops and won't budge, they are not being naughty or misbehaving; they are

afraid of whatever lies ahead. They are trying to communicate to you that they feel scared. Remain calm, work out why they feel afraid, but importantly, NEVER punish a donkey (or any animal for that matter!).

Donkeys don't like the wind and rain, hate having soggy feet and can get very poorly if they eat too much food or become stressed. They will often 'hide' signs that they feel unwell — but if a donkey seems a bit down in the dumps or skips even one meal, it is an emergency to the vet, as they may be a lot more poorly than they are letting on.

Donkeys want to live in their own donkey world — and so we must do everything we can to make sure every interaction is 'donkey friendly'.

HOW TO TALK TO A DONKEY – IT ALL STARTS WITH A SCRATCH!

Talking to donkeys is very similar to talking to horses, however there are some differences. Donkeys like to do what donkeys do naturally! Things like being ridden or lifting their leg for the farrier feel 'unnatural' for donkeys and may take much longer for them to learn than horses and ponies.

When two donkeys groom each other, it is called 'mutual grooming' and is a sign that they are BEST FRIENDS.

Donkeys prefer to be gently scratched on the back rather than stroked or patted! The best way to talk to a donkey and show that we are

their friends is to offer them their favourite donkey things - food, back scratches and the option to hang out with their friends.

THE PET FILES

When donkeys get poorly, they may need to go into donkey hospital. This can be so stressful for them that they stop eating.

However, vets have a trick up their sleeves to tempt them . . .

GINGER BISCUITS!

Horses, ponies and donkeys need lots of fibre from grass and hay to keep their guts and digestion working properly. However, too much lush grass can cause a painful foot condition called laminitis, which is where structures inside the hoof get inflamed or swollen.

Feeding the correct diet is really important, not only to keep them at a healthy weight but also to limit the risk of disease. NEVER offer treats or food to a horse, pony or donkey you don't know.

They may be on a special diet, they might get dangerously poorly and, if nothing else, they might bite! YIKES!

ASK JAMES:
DO UNICORNS EXIST?

Unicorns have captured all our imaginations, but are they real? The truth is — WELL, KIND OF! Fossils show that the extinct 'Siberian unicorn' once walked the earth with humans many thousands of years ago, and it looked a bit like a furry, long-haired rhino crossed with a cow crossed with a giant horse kind of thing. It weighed around a whopping 4 tonnes! But the most distinct finding? A HUGE single horn growing out of its forehead! SO — whilst I can't guarantee the magical white, sparkly mythical unicorns existed, a stockier, less sparkly rhino-horse-cow 'unicorn' creature definitely did! Either way, I think all horses are magic in their own special way. WHOOOOOOSH!

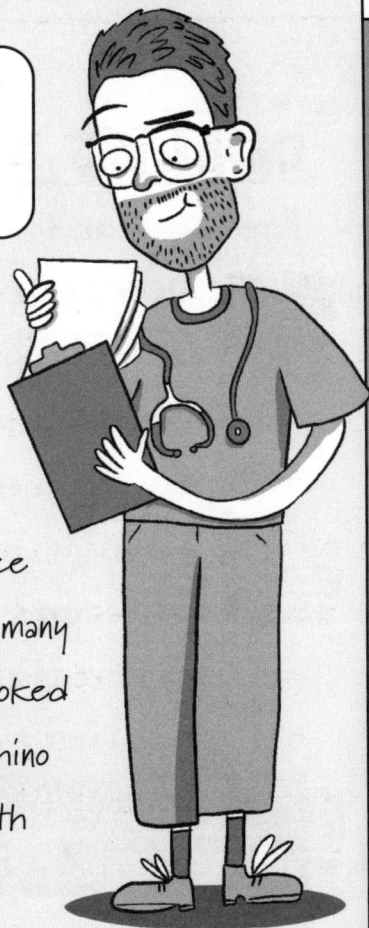

DOLLY'S DOS AND DON'TS

[X] DON'T ever stand directly behind or in front of a horse – always stand on their left-hand side.

[✓] DO use a calm, low voice around horses, ponies and donkeys to let them know you are there.

[✓] DO look from a distance at signs to tell whether a horse is relaxed, happy, dozing or angry BEFORE you approach.

DON'T ever feed a horse, pony or donkey without the owner's permission!

DO give donkeys lots of love – they donkey-deserve it!

I hope you've enjoyed reading all about these amazing pets and how to talk to them. Before we go, it's important to remember that there are some things that EVERY animal wants.

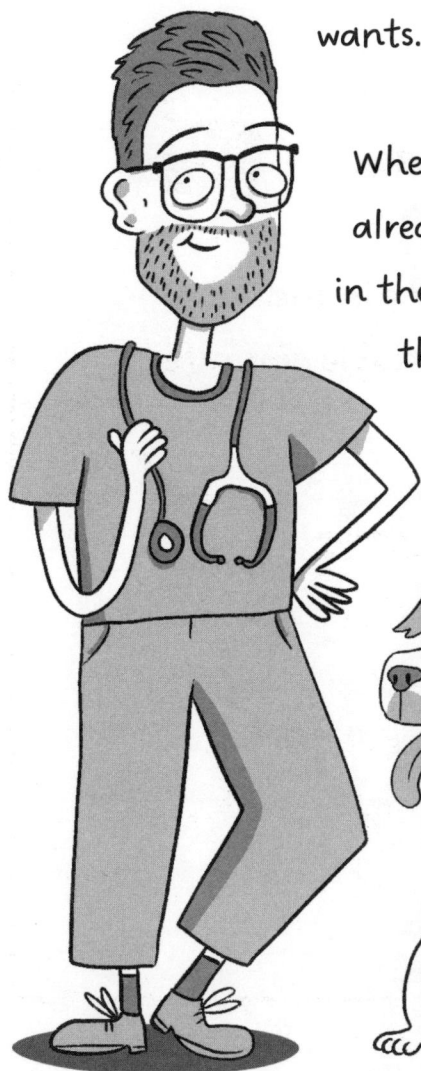

Whether you've got a pet already or are hoping for one in the future, it's helpful to have these five needs in mind. They apply to every single animal you'll ever meet!

DOLLY

NUMBER ONE: GOOD FOOD ☑

It's really important we choose food for our pets that is balanced with all the goodness they need, as well as providing fresh water every day.

NUMBER TWO: CREATURE COMFORTS ☑

All animals like to feel at home in their own type of shelter, with a comfortable and safe place to sleep.

NUMBER THREE: HEALTH ☑

Pets might try to put on a brave face to hide when they're unwell, but like us, they do not enjoy being ill. Keep an eye out for any changes in pet behaviour that might mean they're not feeling their best.

NUMBER FOUR: KEEPING IT NATURAL

Animals like to do what comes naturally: cats want to hunt, dogs want to sniff, rabbits want to dig, slugs want to slime, parrots want to fly. If they can't, they get frustrated. We need to let our pet animals just be animals! (Wait, how did a slug get in there?)

NUMBER FIVE: SAFETY

Dogs, cats, fish, rabbits – all animals are at their happiest when they feel safe. But sometimes animals can feel scared. We should never use fear to 'train' our pets or talk to them with hurtful or loud voices. We must always treat animals with kindness.

Taking on a pet is a **HUGE** responsibility. It is important to always make sure we meet the basic needs of our pets, but really I think we should go further – by listening and talking to our pets, we can work out exactly what they are trying to tell us and we can give them exactly what they want in return! That way, they can truly thrive, and we can relax, knowing they are enjoying their absolute best life!

AUTHOR BIO

Dr James Greenwood is a practising vet and star of CBBC's BAFTA-nominated *The Pets Factor* and Channel 4's *Fur Babies*, as well as being resident vet on BBC One's flagship show *Morning Live*.

His mission is to inspire the younger generation of pet owners to understand the needs and wants of their pets, and to explore how we can live alongside animals and give them the respect and love that they deserve.

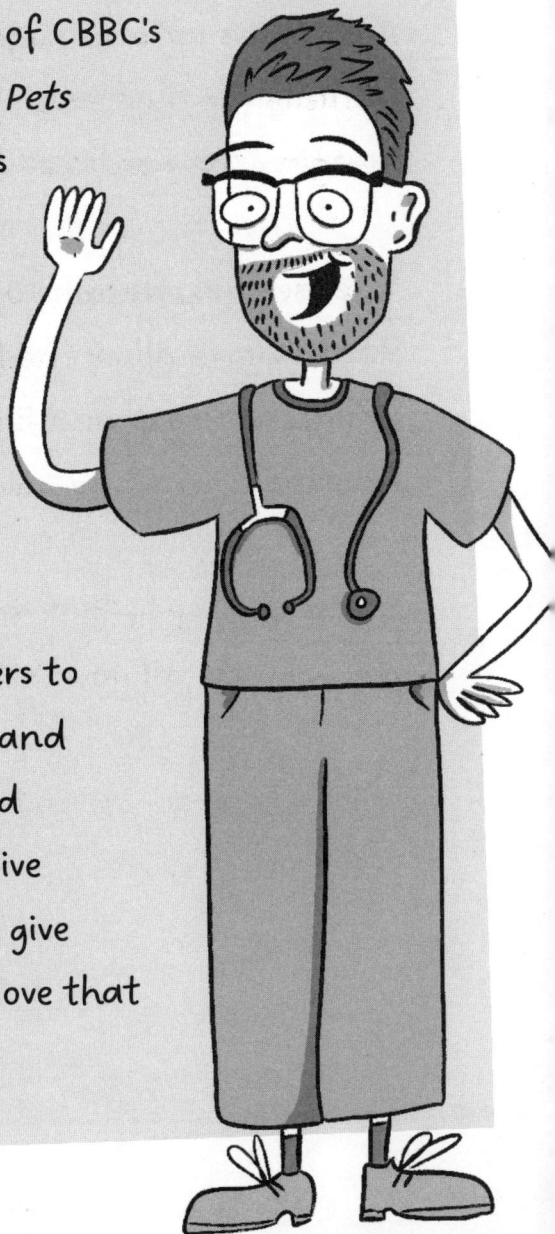

ACKNOWLEDGEMENTS

A big 'paws up' and huge thanks to Rosie and Danielle for their expertise and to Jack for bringing the words to life.

To Rosemary, Natalia, Jonny, Pip and Victoria, and all of the teams at Hachette Children's Group and Encanta, for all your encouragement and guidance – thank you.

And a big wiggly-butt-scratch to my bestest pal Dolly for all your help too!

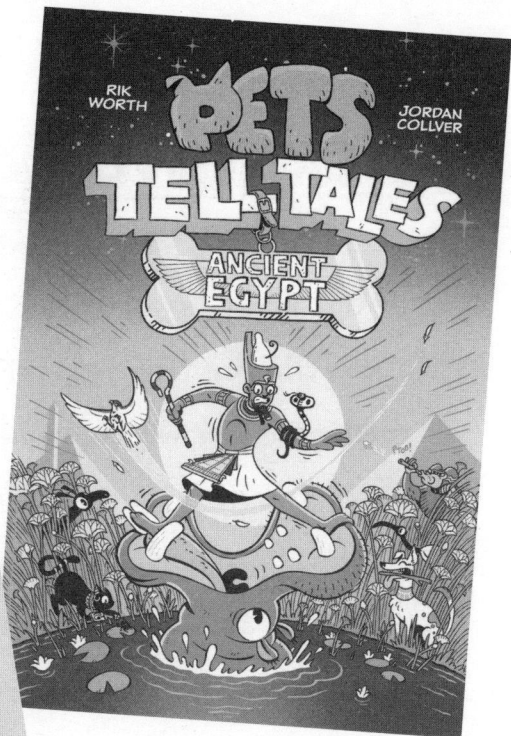

IF YOU LIKED THIS, WHY NOT TRY . . .

wren &rook